D1138919

Geography and Air Transport

Geography and Air Transport

BRIAN GRAHAM
University of Ulster at Coleraine, Northern Ireland

JOHN WILEY & SONS

Chichester · New York · Brisbane · Toronto · Singapore

Published in 1995 John Wiley & Sons Ltd,
                   Baffins Lane, Chichester,
                   West Sussex PO19 1UD, England

                   National   01243 779777
                   International (+44) 1243 779777

Other Wiley Editorial Offices

John Wiley & Sons, Inc., 605 Third Avenue,
New York, NY 10158–0012, USA

Jacaranda Wiley Ltd, 33 Park Road, Milton,
Queensland 4064, Australia

John Wiley & Sons (Canada) Ltd, 22 Worcester Road,
Rexdale, Ontario M9W 1L1, Canada

John Wiley & Sons (SEA) Pte Ltd, 37 Jalan Pemimpin #05–04,
Block B, Union Industrial Building, Singapore 2057

British Library Cataloguing in Publication Data

A catalogue record for this book is available from the British Library

ISBN 0 471 95757 7

Typeset in 10/12pt Palatino by Dorwyn Ltd, Rowlands Castle, Hants
Printed and bound in Great Britain by Bookcraft, Midsomer Norton
This book is printed on acid-free paper responsibly manufactured from sustainable forestation,
for which at least two trees are planted for each one used for paper production.

Contents

To Valerie, Peter and Michael

Preface

The purpose of this book is to provide an interpretation of the geography of the contemporary air transport industry. It is now almost 30 years since the second edition of K. R. Sealy's *Geography of Air Transport* was published. During the intervening period, the structure of air transport has changed dramatically as it responds to deregulatory legislation, aimed at stimulating a more competitive and profitable industry. The geography of route networks has altered significantly, while the industry's scale of operations is now moving away from that of national carriers towards the formation of a number of global airline systems, created by alliances of major operators. The book attempts to chart these developments, placing them in their historical context and seeking to explain regional differences in the application of deregulatory policies. It is concerned too that air transport be interpreted, not as a self-contained industry, but as a mode that cannot be understood apart from the social, political, economic and historical interconnections that created it and, upon which it has significant impacts.

I am indebted to a number of people who have helped me in writing the book. Nigel Dennis, Claire Guyer, Mark Hart, Barry Humphreys and Richard Knowles have kindly commented on various chapters, and I found their comments both stimulating and refreshing. I am grateful to my Head of School, David Eastwood, for his consistent support and encouragement and to my colleagues, particularly Chris Edwards, John Pollard and Mike Poole, for their forbearance while I was writing the book. Anne Hayes typed most of the text and I am indebted to her skill and good humour. Mary Mc-Camphill, Pam Ramsey and Shirley Morrow also gave me valuable assistance. My thanks, too, must go to Kilian McDaid, Nigel McDowell and Mark Millar for their skilful rendition of the diagrams. Peter Graham prepared the references. Much gratitude is also due to Iain Stevenson and his colleagues at John Wiley for all their support and encouragement.

Finally, but above all, I would like to thank my wife, Valerie, who not only read and commented on the entire script but gave me endless support and encouragement through the long months of writing.

Brian Graham
January 1995

Introduction

AIR TRANSPORT IN AN AGE OF ECONOMIC LIBERALISM

This book is concerned with commercial air transport, the particular focus of attention being the world's airline industry. For those who can afford to purchase its products, air transport's distinguishing feature lies in its un-challenged capacity to overcome the friction of time-distance. Any two cities on the planet can now be linked with—at most—one refuelling stop by a fully laden long-range airliner. Even short domestic flights radically lessen journey times between cities compared to other transport modes (although the advantages may be eroded by the time consumed travelling to and from airports). A typical 600-kilometre sector requires about one hour's flying time. Essentially a commodity, air transport masquerades as a supposedly glamorous symbol of the late-twentieth-century obsessions with speed, time-saving and overt displays of consumerism to advertise self-perceptions of status. The industry plays upon its somewhat tawdry charisma in the sexist images and inflated prices with which it confronts the travelling pub-lic. Behind this façade, however, air transport is primarily a service industry, subject, like any other, to a complex of political, economic and social constraints.

As a business, it has two notable characteristics. First, even when profit-able, the air transport business produces only modest returns on capital invested. Because the industry is dependent upon aircraft manufacturing, one of the most complex—and expensive—modern technologies, it is highly capital-intensive. Despite the poor economic returns, the glamorous image of the business has always lured entrepreneurial investors, seduced by the prestige of owning or controlling an airline (Dempsey and Goetz, 1992). Secondly, ever since its origins in the early 1920s, commercial air transport has also attracted an unusual extent of government control and regulation (Lyth, 1993). In the United States, for example, no major business was ever subjected to such detailed daily regulation by the federal government as were the airlines prior to 1978, when that degree of control was swept away by legislation that instituted a new global order for the airline industry (National Commission, 1993).

These changes are symbolic of the ascendancy throughout the contempo-rary capitalist world of neo-liberal (or neo-classical) economic ideologies, committed to ending a previous orthodoxy that envisaged some form of public–private articulation of economies. The key principles of neo-liberalism include the primacy of the market and profit and the enhance-ment of competition, achieved by denationalisation and privatisation of state-owned companies and, above all, by deregulation—the removal, or restructuring, of the regulatory apparatus applied to business structures and practices. Simultaneously, however, the rapidly escalating interdependence of the world-economy means that the economic well-being of individual states is increasingly determined, less by national governments than by complex economic interactions occurring at a global scale (Knox and Agnew, 1994). Economic liberalism has been accompanied by globalisation.

The central concern of the book is to evaluate the effects of an array of neo-liberal policies, currently being applied to the air transport industry world-wide. Much of the recent literature on the business has been written from the perspective of researchers who accept the ideological primacy of market forces and who visualise the air transport industry as a suitable laboratory for their ideas. More widely, this reflects the propagation of market econ-omics as a self-legitimating process that expresses belief in the universal applicability and rationality of the Western development project (Slater, 1993). Contemporary strategies applied to air transport include privatisation of airlines, accompanied by the removal of regulation over such factors as the routes which airlines fly, the tariff structures adopted and the capacities of the aircraft used.

However, the implementation of such policies has produced numerous conflicts of interest. In policy-making terms, aviation should not be ring-fenced and considered in isolation, although in practice it often is. Within such narrow confines, neo-liberal policies lead to inequivalencies between consumers, who desire cost and service benefits from deregulation, and producers interested, not in competition as such but in establishing spatial monopolies through the manipulation and subversion of competitive pro-cesses. More broadly and realistically, all transport systems are dynamic entities that cannot be understood apart from the interconnections of tech-nology, political policies, trade patterns, environment, economics, demogra-phy and historical processes that created them (Hoyle and Smith, 1992). Spatially and ideologically, far more extensive policy issues are involved than the balance of consumer and producer interests on factors such as tariffs and frequency of service. The air transport industry is indivisible from national interests because air travel is more than a mere commodity, sold for consumer gratification. Rather, it is closely linked to strategies addressing socio-economic development and welfare at regional, national and global scales. Spatial variations in air transport provision, and access to it, are thus related to issues of equity, social justice and uneven development within, and between, societies. Arguably, therefore, policy objectives for the indus-try, in attempting to balance the public–private dichotomy, should seek to accomplish social and economic goals beyond mere allocative efficiency (Dempsey, 1989a).

Furthermore, air transport also has to be understood within an historical framework, given that networks evolved to serve purposes different from those which they are now expected to fulfil. Political sovereignty is three-dimensional, extending to the ground beneath and the airspace above states. Air boundaries are subject to the same priorities of defence as are their terrestrial counterparts. Adequately functioning transport infrastructures are inherently important in effecting national integration and in the exercise of international power relationships. Consequently, transport 'is an essential element of both the theory and practice of the spatial development of a nation' (Leinbach and Sien, 1989, p.3). The world's airline networks developed within this context, primarily to serve national interests, and their contemporary geography remains controlled by inter-governmental bilateral agreements.

Inevitably, the provision of air transport services remains tied to these shifting national interests. But further conflicts arise because a succession of disparate national air transport structures and networks is incompatible with the economic forces of internationalisation to which the business is increasingly exposed. The geography of air transport is being restructured through the interplay of the, often antagonistic, forces of deregulation, globalisation and national interest. While air transport largely remains governed at the national level, even under deregulatory regimes, national airlines, operating networks serving national needs, are being superseded by very large companies—the mega-carriers, or by alliances of operators aiming to create pan-global networks. Neo-liberal economic principles have unleashed forces of change which even recalcitrant operators and countries have to respect, even if their reactions are fundamentally defensive. But on every side, the policy tensions remain overt. How can these abrupt, rapidly accelerating and often bewildering changes in the industrial structure and network geography of air transport be reconciled with national interests in sovereignty, employment and regional development? Everywhere, governments often ineptly seek to apply strategies for air transport that attempt to implement neo-liberal economic principles, which inevitably promote internationalisation, while minimising their negative repercussions upon national interests.

THE ARGUMENT OF THE BOOK

In discussing the geography of air transport from this political and economic perspective, the book's argument is concerned to evaluate a set of recurrent themes related to the feasibility of an international air transport industry that is primarily responsive to market forces. These include: the suite of neo-liberal policies—competition, deregulation, privatisation; regional variations in the application and subsequent repercussions of free-market policies; the concurrent transformation of the industry through processes of internationalisation; the ensuing conflicts of interest with policies promoting national well-being. Given the contested nature of the evidence concerning the positive and deleterious effects of the application of neo-liberal principles to the industry, it is perhaps necessary to outline the argument that, hopefully, unifies the text.

It is accepted that the balance of evidence points to the realisation of significant short-term consumer benefits from increased competition in air transport. These include lower fares for some categories of passengers, improved frequencies of services and better connections. Privatisation is something of an adjunct to this process, the principal gains stemming from enhanced competition which in turn makes companies more attractive to investors. However, major tensions are also apparent. Although competition produces more efficient airline management and route networks, while contributing consumer benefits, it also lowers load factors on aircraft and increases their service frequency, thereby augmenting pressures on scarce, expensive and publicly funded air transport infrastructure. Further, as the propensity to fly is positively correlated with Gross National Product (GNP) and disposable income, air transport is an élitist mode of transport, consumer gains from neo-liberal policies accruing to those who already have most. Powerful airlines have also evolved a set of strategies, culminating in the processes of global concentration apparent within the industry, which aim to minimise the pro-competition policies of legislators and call into question the prolongation of consumer benefits. Such processes undermine the rationale of leaving an industry, one that is central to public interest, to unregulated market forces. As Dempsey (1990, p.62) argues, air transport has 'too vast a social and economic impact . . . to leave it to the whims of a dwindling club of unconstrained monopolists'.

Moreover, transport is one pre-requisite among many in alleviating the social and economic consequences of uneven development at regional, national and global scales. Thus, unfettered free-market policies are at variance with notions of equity, social justice and even political expediency. International multilateralism—or free trade—in air transport (opening all markets to all airlines irrespective of their national origins) is to the benefit only of large populous countries, particularly the United States, or small, wealthy countries like Singapore or the Netherlands, whose airlines must expand globally because of the restricted size of their domestic markets. In between lies a diversity of countries—and airlines—which stands to lose as much as it might gain from the uncontrolled application of neo-liberal economics to airline services. Given that the consumer benefits of airline competition are liable to accrue to those who are already most wealthy and that free-market forces are likely to erode the social benefits of air transport and exacerbate regional and global inequalities in income and opportunity, the book argues for a retention of regulatory devices applying to the structure and conduct of the airline business and to consumer behaviour. Ultimately, it maintains, there is a pronounced improbability concerning the ultimate efficacy of unconstrained market economics in commercial air transport.

THE PLAN OF THE BOOK

In elaborating this argument, the book is divided into three parts. Initially, five chapters examine the patterns of global air transport, the nature of air transport markets, the geopolitics and economics of the industry and, finally, its evolving internationalisation and relationship to patterns of uneven development. Part Two addresses the regional implications of these general processes. Chapters 6 and 7 are concerned with the deregulated US airline industry, while Chapters 8 and 9 examine the policies for, and repercussions of, air transport liberalisation in Europe. Chapter 10 deals with the North Atlantic, the principal international market, while Chapters 11 and 12 analyse Asia-Pacific, the world's most dynamic aviation market. Finally, Chapter 13 assesses the difficulties faced by the air transport industries of the Middle East, Africa and Latin America within the new world order. Part Three is devoted to the externalities of air transport, particularly the demands for airport infrastructure and the problem of environmental pollution. Having considered the air transport industry globally, the Conclusion attempts to justify the argument posed above.

One final point concerns the use of acronyms. In common usage, most airlines are referred to by shortened names, readily understood by the general reader and, where possible, used here. In several instances, however, companies are referred to by acronyms as are many institutions and measures connected with air transport. These are defined at first point of usage in the text and all acronyms are listed in Appendix 1. Appendix 2 includes details of the principal commercial transport aircraft (over 80 seats) in current production/service.

Part I

1 Historical Processes and Contemporary Patterns in Air Transport

It is salutary to recall that the history of powered flight is still encompassed within a single century. In that time, aircraft technology has evolved from the first tentative 12-second flight of the *Wright Flyer* at Kitty Hawk, North Carolina, in December 1903, to the B747–400 or A340, capable of flying full passenger loads, non-stop, half-way round the globe. These quite dramatic advances in air transport's capacity to overcome the friction of time and distance have made it the paramount mode of long-distance passenger travel, both between and within countries. By eradicating the effects of maritime, mountain and desert barriers, the industry's development has radically altered patterns of global accessibility. However, air transport remains a high-cost, and thus élitist, form of travel, access to which is largely restricted to the citizens of the world's wealthiest countries. Even within these, the origins of mass air travel date back no further than *circa* 1960. This chapter provides a context for the more detailed discussions that follow in the remainder of the book. It addresses the inter-linked political and technological processes that account for the historical evolution of commercial air transport and describes the contemporary distribution of air traffic.

THE HISTORICAL DEVELOPMENT OF THE AIR TRANSPORT INDUSTRY

The development of air transport as one manifestation of the 20th-century global growth in service industries lacks a substantial recent history. All too often, a concern with the inescapable drama of the pioneering years of civil aviation, particularly those prior to World War II, conceals the economic, social and political frameworks within which the industry developed. Moreover, civil aviation history is often written by aircraft enthusiasts whose concern with technology—and personality—obscures the more fundamental motivations of national and commercial interest that underlie the development of commercial air transport. The earlier social history of the industry is adequately discussed by Hudson and Pettifer (1979), while Sampson (1984) is more overtly concerned with the national ambitions, so vital to an understanding of the airline industry's record. Both books, however, largely pre-date the substantial changes of the past two decades, during which the global air transport industry has been transformed by the combined forces of economic liberalism and internationalisation.

With these exceptions, the inadequacies of general histories of air transport are replicated by those of individual companies. Indeed, it is difficult to cite a single serious business history of an airline. Books belonging to this genre, including Reed's remarkably uncritical account of British Airways (BA) (1990), and Young's more interesting but partisan study of the Hong Kong-based carrier, Cathay Pacific (1988), are all too often little more than hagiographies. Airline history is interpreted from the perspective of the 'legendary' entrepreneurial figures of the industry such as Juan Trippe, who ran Pan American for 40 years, or Sir Freddie Laker, often depicted as the man who opened up the North Atlantic market and the martyr-hero of the latter-day deregulators. Yet the basic behavioural questions surrounding entrepreneurial investment into an industry characterised by low and wildly fluctuating returns on capital remain as yet unanswered (Lyth, 1993). Again, the often murky relationships between those dominant aviation personalities and their respective governments require detailed examination.

Although airships were used on internal routes in Germany prior to World War I, commercial international flights began only in 1919 with the inauguration of the first services between London (initially served by Hounslow and then Croydon) and Paris Le Bourget. During the 1920s, intra-European route networks were gradually established, while trans-Mediterranean services to North Africa got underway. From the outset, it was apparent that passenger traffic was not in itself sufficiently profitable to support air transport as a mode of travel. Some form of government subsidy, usually in the form of airmail contracts, was also necessary. Indeed, the initial development of commercial air transport in Europe was far more dependent on mail than on passengers, one important reason explaining the ubiquitous nature of subsequent government regulation of the industry.

The same is true of the United States where the Post Office founded an airmail service in 1919. In 1925, this was handed over to private carriers on a tendering basis, creating the network structure from which the principal passenger-carrying airlines soon evolved. In 1930, transcontinental air travel took 36 hours, with 10 stops and an overnight rest at Kansas City. Only two years later, advances in night-flying techniques had eliminated the stop-over and reduced the New York–Los Angeles trip to 24 hours (Hudson and Pettifer, 1979). Even then, it was apparent that significant advantages were conferred upon US airlines by the large, politically and geographically unified, continental domestic market within which they were operating. More than any other factor, this was to allow US airline and aerospace industries to develop on a scale that a politically fragmented Europe could never emulate. In many respects, the geography of contemporary US airline networks still reflects the shape of the original airmail route systems (see Dempsey and Goetz, 1992, which contains an excellent summary of the historical evolution of the major US carriers).

From its earliest beginnings, therefore, the development of commercial air transport has to be interpreted within a context of national interests, a factor that remains a potent influence upon the contemporary patterning of the industry. An interlocking nexus of mail, empire and administration motivated early attempts at developing intercontinental air transport during the 1920s. Its pioneers encountered major technological pitfalls in aircraft, equipped with only the most primitive navigational instruments, and lacking sufficient endurance for long over-water flights, as well as the altitudinal capacity to cross the higher mountain ranges. In addition, night-landings were very difficult, early methods depending on no more than flares to guide the aircraft in. Thus, while it is important not to let the romance and dangers of pioneering flight subsume the business history of the air transport industry, the achievements of early pilots must still be recognised for the feats of bravery that they were.

The great pioneering solo flights, most famously Charles Lindbergh's 1927 solo west–east transatlantic crossing in the *Spirit of St. Louis*, captured the American and European popular imagination and did much for the prospects of international air travel (Sampson, 1984). Jean Mermoz, foremost among the pilots to develop the Latécoère company's 'Line', the French mail service between Toulouse, Casablanca and Dakar, was another great pioneer of civil aviation. Forced along the fringe of Atlantic Africa by the desert, the 'Line's' pilots and their fragile aircraft depended on a chain of forts strung along the coast. Immortalised in Antoine de Saint-Exupéry's *Wind, Sand and Stars* (1939), one of the very few works of literature to emerge from the usually prosaic world of air transport, Mermoz crossed the Andes in 1928 and then, in 1930, flew Aéropostale's first airmail service across the South Atlantic between St. Louis, Senegal, and Natal, Brazil. By 1931, it took only four days for mail to travel from Toulouse to Buenos Aires. It was dangerous work though: having pioneered 'the desert, the mountains, the night and the sea', Mermoz disappeared over the South Atlantic. Saint-Exupéry's images of bravery, freedom and fellowship, of man and flimsy machine battling against Nature and the eternity 'that lies below the sea of clouds', remain fundamental to that sense of adventure, and even occasional danger, that distantly connects contemporary commercial air transport to its more romantic origins.

Latin American networks were built up by both European and North American intervention. Luft Hansa (as it then was) joined Aéropostale in the development of services across the South Atlantic. Germany's important commercial interests in Latin America led to investments in airlines including the Brazilian carrier, Varig, and the predecessors of Colombia's Avianca. Pan American, soon to become the pre-eminent US international airline, and often referred to as 'the other State Department' (Dempsey and Goetz, 1992), was founded in 1928. The carrier rapidly developed an airmail network throughout Latin America, Lindbergh himself pioneering many of the routes. The US government, determined to protect its political and commercial interests in Latin America and the Caribbean against German, French and Italian influences, strongly supported these developments.

During the early 1930s, passenger services began to evolve upon this initial framework of mail routes. Those between Casablanca and Dakar did not begin until 1936, following the consolidation of the French mail lines into Air France in 1933. One of these carriers, Air Orient, which operated between Paris and Saigon, was among a number of airlines responsible for opening up the routes between Europe, Africa and Asia. Other key pioneers included the Dutch carrier, KLM, and Britain's Imperial Airways. Mail continued to be a principal *raison d'être* behind these ventures, although national ambitions and the geography of empire were further crucial motivations. KLM, which claims to be the world's oldest continuously operating airline, developed the routes between the Netherlands and the Dutch East Indies (now Indonesia), by 1931 the world's longest scheduled airline flight. In turn Imperial Airways (later to become BOAC, one of the precursors of BA) connected Britain with its Middle East dependencies, African and Asian colonies and Australia (Figure 1.1).

Neither the routes to South Africa or Asia, although very long, offered the same technological challenges encountered in the pioneering of transoceanic services. Imperial's Cairo–Cape service to Kenya, Rhodesia and South Africa, which began in April 1932, used flying boats to exploit the route down the Nile and African Rift Valley. As this passed east of the Sahara, it presented fewer physical barriers to aircraft than did the French route to West Africa. The airline's Asian service reached Singapore in 1934 where it connected with the Australian airline, Qantas, to link London with Brisbane and then Sydney. Travellers flew from Croydon to Paris, hence by train to Brindisi in Italy (until 1936, Mussolini would not permit overflying of Italian territory). A combination of sea- and land-planes required more than 30 stages to connect Brindisi with Brisbane, the handful of travellers staying overnight at hotels *en route*. Even by the mid 1930s, some of the planes used on these services could carry only around a dozen passengers, (Frater, 1986, provides an entertaining account). As late as 1938, when the service was being operated by the Empire flying boats, which could carry up to 24 passengers, the journey between Southampton and Sydney still required nine and a half days' flying time. By then, Pan American was also opening up transpacific services, while the first revenue flights across the North Atlantic began in 1939.

The rapid evolution of this first phase of intercontinental air transport was interrupted by World War II, although, paradoxically, this provided a tremendous impetus to the development of all aspects of aircraft technology. The economic and physical costs of the war in Europe meant that the United

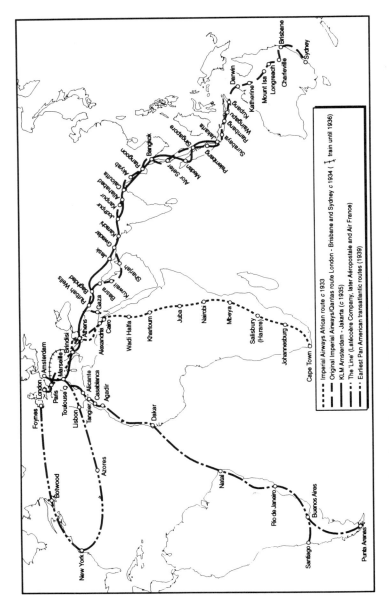

Figure 1.1. Some major pioneering intercontinental air routes
Based on information in Hudson and Pettifer, 1979; Sampson, 1984; Frater, 1986

States, already benefiting from its large domestic market, emerged after 1945 as by far the strongest civil aviation power world-wide. Indeed, the initiative in civil aviation had already passed irretrievably from Europe to the United States prior to 1939, symbolised by the development of the all-metal Douglas DC-2 and, more famously, DC-3, the first planes on which airlines could make profits from passengers alone (Lyth, 1993).

To some extent, the post-war era can be subdivided into periods defined by major advances in aircraft technology. Up to 1958, international air transport was dominated by four-engined piston and turbo-prop airliners, the most successful commercial designs coming from Boeing, Douglas and Lockheed. The first jet passenger aircraft—the British de Havilland Comet—entered service in 1952, but a succession of fatal crashes, caused by inadequate understanding of pressurisation, led to it being grounded Thus, the jet age effectively began only in 1958 when the intercontinental B707 and DC-8 both entered service. The rush for speed became the dominant motivation in the airline business and, during the 1960s, a succession of short-range jet types began to replace the turbo-props on domestic and international routes. Since 1970, aircraft technology has been dominated by three interconnected factors—increases in passenger and cargo capacity, the quest for extended range and the continued development of the turbo-fan engine. The first four-engined wide-bodied aircraft, the B747 (later variants of which can carry in excess of 600 passengers) entered passenger service with Pan American in 1970, later followed by the DC-10 and L-1011 tri-jets. Subsequent developments in engine technology now permit wide-bodies to travel over markedly extended ranges. Even more important commercially, most of the newer-generation aircraft require only two engines (see Appendix 2).

Nevertheless, no matter how vital the contribution of technology has been to the rapid evolution of commercial air transport, it remains a permissive effect rather than an explanation of the industry's growth. Instead of initiating change, technological developments have emanated from airline demands for capacity, speed and range. At one level, these requirements reflect the marked increase in disposable income per capita, characteristic of the developed world from the late 1950s onwards. This factor dramatically enhanced the demand for air transport, most notably through the changes which it induced in the leisure behaviour of wealthier countries.

The resultant widening of the industry's consumer base has been the most significant contemporary change in the sociology of air transport. As recently as 1960, air traffic was split more or less equally between business and leisure markets. By 1980, however, two-thirds of all air travellers were flying for leisure reasons, a proportion that has now increased to around 70 per cent. The Inclusive Tour (IT) concept, first introduced in Britain during the late 1950s, combines fare, hotel accommodation, meals and transit costs in one package price. Its development was entirely conditional upon the availability of air transport, an independent, or charter, airline sector soon emerging in response to the demand created by this market. To take but one example of its effect upon destination countries, visitor arrivals in Spain, the most important IT market, increased from 1.5 million in 1952 to 42.9 million in 1984 (Lyth and Dierikx, 1994). Although the IT concept radically enlarged the demand for air travel, and altered the structure of the industry through the development of dedicated charter airlines, the scheduled carriers were also forced to come to terms with the rise of the leisure market, particularly on intercontinental routes. During the 1970s, for example, the entry of Laker's 'Skytrain' services into the most important international market, the North Atlantic, forced the traditional scheduled airlines to offer competing and much enhanced fare structures, a legacy that survived Laker's bankruptcy in 1982 (see Chapter 10).

The growth of the leisure sector in air transport graphically illustrates the very precise relationship between demand for air services and disposable income. Both within and between countries, there is a clear correlation between high income and most travelled, and low income and least travelled, by air (see Chapter 2). At the global scale, therefore, the age of mass air travel is restricted geographically to only three regions—North America, most of Europe and parts of Asia-Pacific, most notably Japan, the Newly Industrialised Countries (NICs) of the West Pacific Rim and Australasia. Thus, although the customer base for air transport has become markedly more egalitarian within these regions, at the global scale the mode remains the privileged and élitist form of transport that it has always been.

On an entirely different level, the rapid post-war development of commercial air transport is bound up with a complex of interrelated political, economic and technological processes, representative of widespread and revolutionary changes in global social structures. The partial transfer of power from the nation-state to a dynamically interconnected capitalist world-system, the role of global geopolitical power-bloc formations and, more arguably, the spread of a pervasive US cultural hegemony, are all factors that impinge upon the structure of the air transport industry. But so too does the highly unequal spatial patterning of these processes (G. Smith, 1994). As with other geographical phenomena, the demand for air transport can be conceptualised within a framework that attempts to integrate local and global processes (see Chapter 5).

THE CONTEMPORARY DISTRIBUTION OF AIR TRAFFIC

In several important ways, commercial air transport has always been a global industry. The intercontinental routes, pioneered during the late 1920s and 1930s, were concerned with linking world-embracing empires and political spheres of influence. Again, the industry is subject to multilateral international conventions and controlled by pan-global institutions. Foremost among the latter is the International Civil Aviation Organization (ICAO),

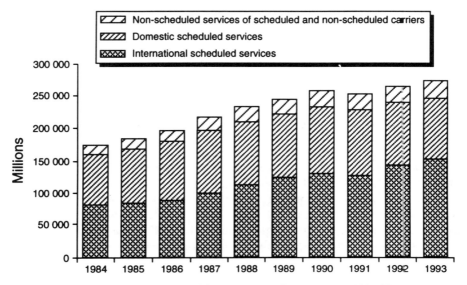

Figure 1.2. Tonne-kms performed by commercial air carriers, 1984–93
Source: ICAO, 1994a

formally established as a United Nations' agency in 1947 to administer international air services. In addition, virtually all scheduled airlines belong to the International Air Transport Association (IATA), which administers fares and cargo rates, acts as a clearing house for airline ticketing, and co-operates with ICAO on the airlines' behalf.

ICAO REGIONS

When reporting statistics relating to airline traffic, ICAO divides the world into six continental regions of carrier registration (Figure 1.3). These are: Africa; Asia-Pacific (including all of Asia south of the Russian border and Australasia); Europe (current data relating to the Commonwealth of Independent States or CIS—the former Soviet Union—cannot be considered reliable); Middle East; North America; Latin America and the Caribbean. With the exception of 1991, when the demand for air travel fell globally, the combined repercussion of recession, the Iraqi invasion of Kuwait and the subsequent Gulf War, the supply of both scheduled and non-scheduled air services has grown steadily over the past decade (Figure 1.2). Measured by tonne-kilometres performed, the provision of international scheduled services doubled between 1984–93, while that of domestic services increased by around 40 per cent. Non-scheduled services also displayed substantial growth, recording a 67 per cent increase over the 10-year period.

Table 1.1. Scheduled traffic of commercial air carriers, 1993 (total tonne-km performed by ICAO region of carrier registration)

ICAO statistical region of carrier registration	Total tonne-km performed (millions)	Percentage of total tonne-km performed
Europe (including CIS)	68 005	27.28
Africa	5 178	2.08
Middle East	8 295	3.33
Asia-Pacific	61 072	24.50
North America	94 768	38.03
Latin America and Caribbean	11 891	4.78
Total	249 209	100.00

Source: ICAO (1994a).

In 1993, the total scheduled traffic carried by the airlines of ICAO Contracting States was almost 250 billion tonne-kms performed. Some 660 airlines carried 1171m passengers and 17.5m tonnes of freight. International traffic accounted for 53 per cent of total passenger-kilometres, 82 per cent of freight tonne-kilometres, and 62 per cent of total tonne-kilometres performed. Due to lack of growth in the US internal market, and a continuing fall in traffic within the CIS, world domestic traffic declined from 98.6 billion tonne-kilometres performed in 1992 to 96.4 billion tonne-kilometres performed in 1993 (ICAO, 1994b). Marked intra-regional variations characterise shares of total world traffic (Table 1.1). In 1992, North America, Europe and Asia-Pacific accounted for virtually 90 per cent of total world scheduled passenger, freight and mail traffic (defined as tonne-kilometres performed). Within this markedly skewed global pattern, around 43 per cent of all scheduled passenger, mail and freight traffic was carried by the airlines of only two countries, the United States and the United Kingdom (36 and seven per cent respectively). Not surprisingly, virtually all the top-ranked countries for scheduled air traffic are located within North America, Europe and Asia-Pacific (Table 1.2). The carriers of these states accounted for over 85 per cent of total scheduled tonne-kilometres performed during 1993.

Among other factors, the large percentage of traffic carried by North American carriers reflects the size and domestic nature of the bulk of their market. The highest share of international passenger scheduled traffic—around 34 per cent—is carried by European airlines, which also account for the largest single component of the world charter market. Non-scheduled traffic accounted for 15 per cent of overall international passenger traffic in 1993, almost two-thirds being handled by specialist non-scheduled operators. Such statistics reflect the distribution of demand for international air transport. While North America is the largest single market, it is largely a domestic one. In contrast, political fragmentation and economic wealth

Table 1.2. Top 20 countries, total tonne-km performed on scheduled services by ICAO states, 1993

Rank in 1993	Country	Estimated total tonne-km performed (millions)	Percentage of total tonne-km performed
1	United States	89 845	35.76
2	United Kingdom	17 427	6.94
3	Japan	14 679	5.84
4	CIS[a]	10 870	4.33
5	Germany	10 116	4.03
6	France	9 612	3.83
7	Australia	7 806	3.11
8	South Korea	7 191	2.86
9	Singapore	6 714	2.67
10	Netherlands	6 388	2.54
11	Canada	5 138	2.04
12	China	4 760	1.89
13	Brazil	4 152	1.65
14	Italy	4 030	1.60
15	Thailand	3 164	1.26
16	Spain	3 018	1.20
17	Switzerland	2 982	1.19
18	Scandinavia[b]	2 598	1.03
19	Saudi Arabia	2 400	0.96
20	Indonesia	2 340	0.93

[a] Eleven CIS states that are ICAO Contracting States.
[b] Denmark, Norway and Sweden which share one national airline.
Source: ICAO (1994b, p.14).

ensure that intra-European services constitute by far the most substantial international market, accounting for about one-third of all scheduled international passengers carried on IATA airlines during 1993. Intra-Asian-Pacific traffic and the North Atlantic contributed around 15 and 12 per cent of international traffic respectively (Figure 1.3).

PRINCIPAL AIRLINES AND CITY-PAIRINGS

Not surprisingly, the world distribution of major airline operators correlates markedly with the regional traffic patterns shown in Table 1.2. Airline productivity is commonly measured by several indices which, inevitably, tend to produce different rank orders. However, excepting only international scheduled passenger traffic, US airlines dominate every listing, while virtually all the carriers included are registered in North American, European or Asian-Pacific countries. For example, of the world's top 30 scheduled airline groups in 1993, ranked by sales (which includes non-airline activities), only two—Saudi Arabian Airlines (Saudia) and Varig—are based in countries outside these regions (Table 1.3). No less than six of the top 11

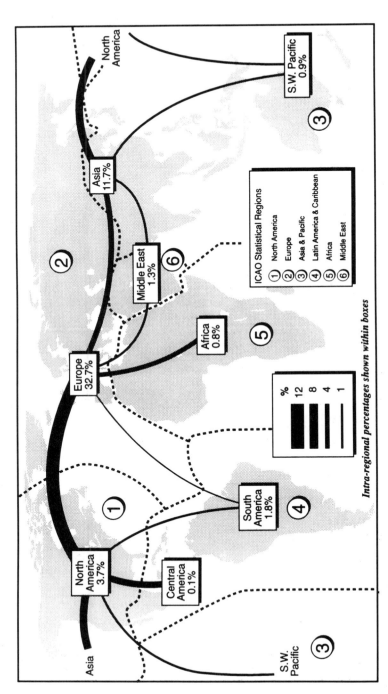

Figure 1.3. Principal international air traffic flows, 1993 (percentage IATA scheduled international passengers). Boxes show traffic within regions

Source: IATA, 1994

airlines in this particular ranking are US-domiciled. Table 1.4, snowing the top 25 airlines by scheduled passenger traffic in 1993, has an even more pronounced bias, BA being the sole non-US carrier in the top seven places.

The US hegemony is disturbed only when international passenger traffic statistics are considered separately (Table 1.5). Not surprisingly, European and Asian-Pacific airlines are more dominant in international passenger traffic, reflecting the political fragmentation of their home regions and the restricted spatial extent of certain domestic markets. Two airlines in particular, Singapore Airlines and Cathay Pacific, are entirely dependent on international traffic. With the exception of Federal Express (FedEx) and Northwest, the most important freight carriers are also European or Asian-Pacific airlines (see Table 2.2).

Table 1.3. World's top 30 scheduled airline groups by sales, 1993

Rank 1993	Airline group	Country	Sales in (US$ m)
1	American (AMR)	USA	15 816
2	United	USA	14 511
3	Delta	USA	12 295
4	Lufthansa	Germany	10 746
5	*Groupe* Air France	France	9 728
6	BA	UK	9 550
7	JAL	Japan	9 160
8	Northwest	USA	8 649
9	All Nippon	Japan	7 224
10	USAir Group	USA	7 083
11	Continental	USA	5 775
12	SAS	Denmark/Norway/Sweden	4 996
13	Alitalia	Italy	4 642
14	KLM	Netherlands	4 613
15	Swissair	Switzerland	4 326
16	Qantas	Australia	4 060
17	Singapore	Singapore	3 898
18	Iberia	Spain	3 308
19	Korean	S Korea	3 342
20	TWA	USA	3 157
21	Cathay Pacific	Hong Kong	3 102
22	Air Canada	Canada	2 789
23	Saudia	Saudi Arabia	2 491
24	Japan Air System	Japan	2 533
25	Varig	Brazil	2 517
26	Thai	Thailand	2 312
27	Canadian	Canada	2 305
28	Southwest	USA	2 297
29	Ansett Australia	Australia	2 048
30	Garuda Indonesia	Indonesia	1 784

Source: Flight International (22–8 June 1994).

Table 1.4. Top 25 airlines by scheduled passenger traffic, 1993

Rank	Airline	Total passenger traffic billion revenue (passenger-km)	Passengers carried (millions)	Rank
1	United	162.5	69.7	3
2	American	156.3	82.5	2
3	Delta	133.4	85.0	1
4	Northwest	93.5	44.1	5
5	BA	80.1	28.1	9
6	Continental	68.1	36.6	6
7	USAir	56.7	53.7	4
8	JAL	54.6	24.0	10
9	Lufthansa	47.6	28.8	8
10	Qantas[a]	44.5	12.4	17
11	Air France[b]	43.5	14.4	15
12	Singapore	41.3	9.3	23
13	All Nippon	36.8	33.7	7
14	KLM	36.8	9.9	21
15	TWA	36.7	19.1	12
16	Cathay Pacific	29.1	8.9	24
17	Alitalia	28.4	19.6	11
18	Korean	25.6	16.2	14
19	Iberia	23.3	14.4	15
20	Thai	22.9	10.2	20
21	Varig	21.2	9.7	22
22	Air Canada	20.5	10.7	19
23	Canadian	19.9	6.9	25
24	Saudia	18.6	11.9	18
25	SAS	18.1	18.6	13

[a] Includes Australian
[b] Excludes Air Inter

Source: Flight International (22–8 June 1994), collated from IATA (1994).

If the 1993 rankings for total international scheduled traffic (measured as total tonne-kms performed) are compared to those for 1984, three points are discernible (Table 1.5). First, a number of Asian-Pacific carriers have improved their positions although Japan Airlines (JAL) has suffered a significant decline. This reflects the relatively high growth of traffic in Asia-Pacific generally, currently the world's most dynamic regional economy, but also the severe economic depression in Japan during the early 1990s. Secondly, the US all-freight carrier, FedEx, has advanced from 144th place to 18th, testimony to the recent and explosive growth of the overnight package business (see Chapter 2). Finally, the data also illustrate the dramatic restructuring of the US airline industry following deregulation. Three airlines in particular—American, United and Delta—have emerged as mega-carriers, a strength vested in the extent of their US domestic networks. They

Table 1.5. Top 30 airlines, total international scheduled traffic, 1993

Rank	Carrier	Total tonne-km performed, 1993 (millions)	Ranking 1984
1	BA	10 052	2
2	Lufthansa	9 523	3
3	Air France	7 347	4
4	United	7 304	49
5	JAL	7 034	1
6	Singapore	6 826	7
7	KLM	6 617	6
8	American	5 715	33
9	Northwest	5 508	10
10	Korean	5 399	9
11	Qantas	4 781	11
12	Cathay Pacific	4 523	15
13	Delta	4 165	47
14	Alitalia	3 359	14
15	Thai	2 940	21
16	Swissair	2 934	13
17	Varig	2 181	23
18	Federal Express (FedEx)	2 087	144
19	Iberia	2 063	16
20	Malaysian	1 898	34
21	Saudia	1 816	19
22	Aeroflot	1 764	17
23	SAS	1 702	20
24	Continental	1 702	52
25	Canadian	1 700	31
26	Garuda	1 695	35
27	Air Canada	1 655	18
28	El Al	1 638	24
29	Air New Zealand	1 622	30
30	Philippine	1 478	28

Source: ICAO (1994b, p.12).

have also become important international operators, succeeding Pan American (ranked fifth in 1984), which went bankrupt in 1991, and Trans World Airlines (TWA), the eighth-ranked carrier in 1984 but now locked into a spiral of continuing decline. Of the traditional US international carriers, only Northwest has marginally improved its position.

The major international city-pairings are also concentrated in Europe and Asia-Pacific and on the routes connecting both regions to North America (Table 1.6). A city-pairing includes all the traffic between two cities, irrespective of airports used (a number of major cities are served by more than one airport). Predictably, the busiest international routes occur in only four markets. The first comprises a number of short-haul intra-European city-pairs, all of which include London. Secondly, 13 of the world's top 25 international

Table 1.6. Scheduled passenger traffic on world's most important international city-pairs, year ending September 1992

Rank	City-pair (first-named city generates more traffic)	1992 (000s)	Distance (km)
1	London–Paris	3 402	346
2	London–New York	2 276	5 539
3	Hong Kong–Taipei	2 223	777
4	Honolulu–Tokyo	2 131	6 134
5	Kuala Lumpur–Singapore	2 109	335
6	Seoul–Tokyo	2 023	1 227
7	Hong Kong–Tokyo	2 019	2 938
8	Amsterdam–London	1 775	369
9	Dublin–London	1 720	449
10	Bangkok–Hong Kong	1 649	1 711
11	Jakarta–Singapore	1 381	906
12	Singapore–Tokyo	1 256	5 356
13	Frankfurt–London	1 222	654
14	New York–Paris	1 218	5 833
15	Los Angeles–Tokyo	1 094	8 752
16	Taipei–Tokyo	1 090	2 182
17	London–Los Angeles	1 015	8 759
18	Brussels–London	1 015	349
19	Hong Kong–Manila	998	1 126
20	Hong Kong–Singapore	997	2 578
21	Bangkok–Singapore	982	1 444
22	London–Tokyo	951	9 590
23	London–Zurich	908	787
24	Bangkok–Tokyo	901	4 644
25	Guam Island–Tokyo	858	2 516

Source: ICAO (1994a).

city-pairs fall entirely within Asia-Pacific, while three more terminate within it. Tokyo is the principal node, followed by Hong Kong and Singapore. Finally, there are the busiest transpacific and transatlantic routes. However, because the US domestic market accounts for virtually 40 per cent of all global scheduled passenger air traffic, the global airport rankings are dominated by the principal US domestic terminals and international gateways, 17 of the world's top 30 airports in 1993 being located within the continental United States (see Table 14.1). Conversely, excepting the principal North American gateways—New York (JFK) and Miami—the most important airports for international passenger traffic are exclusively located, either in Europe or around the West Pacific Rim (see Table 14.2).

CONCLUSIONS

The contemporary distribution of air traffic is a reflection of a complex matrix of social, political and economic influences upon market demand.

These will be explored in subsequent chapters in Part One, particular attention being given to the implications of the implementation of competition, privatisation, deregulation and globalisation for the supply of, and demand for, air transport. Clearly, while demand is regionally biased because of global disparities in wealth, there are further spatial variations in government attitudes to the neo-liberal restructuring of the commercial air transport industry. These concerns provide the basis for the regional discussions which form Part Two of the book.

2 Air Transport Markets

The supplier's perspective tends to dominate discussions of demand in the air transport industry. Socio-economic and demographic characteristics of air travellers can be established relatively easily, but compared, for example, with research into urban travel choice decision-making, the behavioural approach to the study of airline networks and flows has been largely ignored (Taaffe and Gauthier, 1994). Again, there is very little evidence of the effectiveness or accuracy of the information flows linking suppliers and consumers of air transport or of the role played by the travel trade in influencing consumer choice. An airline ticket is more than a simple representation of an individual's right to journey on a particular flight. Because there are different classes of travel, the commodity also functions as an expression of perceived social status. There is little evidence to show how firms monitor the costs of air transport or differentiate distance components from those incurred through purchasing more nebulous symbols of prestige.

Given these limitations, it is still possible to establish the basic parameters of consumer demand, three key aspects being isolated in this chapter. First, the segmented nature of both passenger and cargo air transport markets is established. Secondly, an analysis is offered of the socio-economic and demographic factors that determine the consumption of air transport. These are related to characteristics of individual consumers, geographical disparities in development and supplier-led manipulation of markets. Finally, some attention is given to the forecasting of consumer demand for air transport.

MARKET SEGMENTATION

Air travel is a segmented or differentiated product, the nature of that segmentation differing from market to market. Initially, passengers can be divided into those travelling for business or leisure purposes; secondly, the airline business is segmented between passengers and freight, aircraft carrying both simultaneously. For the suppliers of air transport, a precise understanding of traffic segmentation is the key to accurate market share analysis.

PASSENGER SEGMENTATION

Three aspects of journeys by air—purpose, length and type—can be used to define market segmentation of passengers. In turn, these processes are

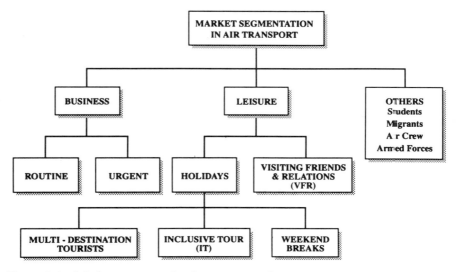

Figure 2.1. Market segmentation in passenger air transport
Based on Doganis, 1991

dependent on the demands for air travel created by the economic, social, demographic and historical characteristics of the markets at either end of the route.

Initially, a business/leisure dichotomy can be used to differentiate journey purpose, a binary classification that distinguishes those passengers who are having their fares paid by employers or clients from those paying their own way. This crude dichotomy can be immediately refined (Figure 2.1). Business travellers, making routine, repeated journeys, can be distinguished from those engaged in urgent, or even emergency, journeys. Leisure travellers are customarily divided between holidaymakers (further split into IT, multi-destination or weekend break sub-segments) and the VFR (visiting friends and relations) market. Finally, some passengers—for example those travelling for educational reasons, members of the armed services, airline staff and migrants, either permanent or temporary—are conventionally grouped as a miscellaneous category because they do not fit clearly into either the business or leisure classifications (Doganis, 1991).

The market segmentation of a particular flight will also depend on the length of journey (Table 2.1). Short-haul routes tend to carry a higher proportion of business travellers than do long-haul, even when the latter link important commercial centres such as London and New York. However, the relationship between market segmentation and journey length is complicated by variations in the historical and contemporary economic, social and demographic characteristics of the city-pairing. For example, business

Table 2.1. London Heathrow routes, 1991: primary market segmentation

London Heathrow (to and from)	Percentage business travellers	Percentage leisure travellers
Short-haul		
Amsterdam	50	50
Brussels	73	26
Dublin	37	63
Frankfurt	51	49
Geneva	44	56
Paris	50	50
Rotterdam	76	23
Zurich	49	51
Long-haul		
Los Angeles	14	86
New York (JFK)	25	75
Newark	28	72

Source: CAA (1993a).

passengers predominate on certain short-haul routes, accounting for around 75 per cent of the London to Rotterdam or Brussels markets. Conversely, leisure traffic accounts for almost two-thirds of London Heathrow–Dublin traffic, reflecting the long-term migration of Irish people to England and the ensuing web of social interrelationships that connects the two countries. More commonly, as in the Heathrow to Paris, Amsterdam, Frankfurt and Zurich markets, there is a relatively equitable split between business and leisure passengers, many of the latter travelling on weekend breaks. In this respect, it can be difficult to distinguish between leisure and business traffic, given that the most important venues globally for international conventions (London, Paris, Geneva and Brussels) are all leading tourist cities (Daniels, 1993).

The precise composition of this segmented marketing mix is crucial to the carriers because profit yield from business passengers is higher than that obtained from those travelling for leisure reasons. (Yield is defined as the operating revenue gained per revenue tonne-km flown.) In airline terms, the mix is likely to improve as a particular service matures. The extent to which yield can rise depends on the economic and social characteristics of the cities at either end of the route and the types of journey being made between them. Airlines provide both point-to-point and connecting services. The former link the passenger's originating and destination cities by non-stop flights. However, as most city-pairings are not linked by direct services, passengers must change aircraft at a third airport. For example, connecting passengers accounted for more than 25 per cent of enplanements at Heathrow in 1991 (CAA, 1993a), a figure that can reach 60 per cent at some major US airports.

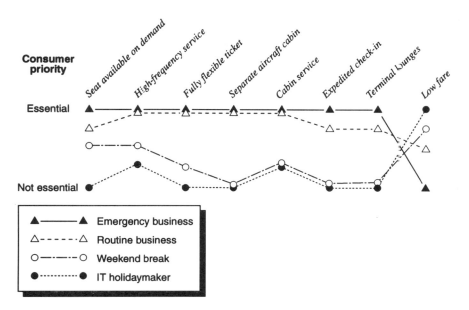

Figure 2.2.   Consumer priorities in passenger air transport
Based on Doganis, 1991

The differing market segments, defined along the business or leisure, short or long haul and point-to-point or connecting axes, present the suppliers with conflicting needs and requirements. Apart from shared concerns such as safety and security, the priorities that are attached to these demands reflect divergent attitudes to price (Figure 2.2). Air travel is highly elastic in income and inelastic in price (Alperovich and Machnes, 1994), a rule qualified, however, by market segmentation. Business travel is relatively price inelastic—that is, the impact of price on demand is limited. Other factors being equal, airlines will simply charge whatever prices the market will bear. Conversely, low-yield leisure traffic is price elastic, small changes in costs having substantial impacts on demand. The problem for the scheduled airline is to combine these different markets in one aircraft.

Business travellers attach a very high priority to needs concerned with schedule convenience: these include punctuality, flexibility of ticketing, high frequency of service and expedited check-in times (S. J. Shaw, 1990). They book late and make multiple reservations because airlines do not penalise cancellation of full-fare tickets. Consequently, they may fail to turn up for flights at all (in airline terminology, the 'no-shows' who may account for 10–15 per cent of the reservations on an average scheduled flight). This is an important element in depressing aircraft load factors. Given the similarity of airline products, the decision-making processes of business travellers may be more influenced by an additional series of 'wants' that include: separate check-ins, lounges and aircraft cabins that indicate status and may offer enhanced working environments; jet (as distinct from turbo-prop) aircraft; a high-status airline offering attractive marketing inducements; good-quality in-flight service and seating comfort; a wide array of connections. These wants will be assigned different priorities, depending on length of journey. For instance, separate cabins, seating comfort, in-flight entertainment and a non-stop service may be the leading priorities for a long-haul flight.

In contrast, few of these factors are important to a leisure trade dominated by price, the largest market share going to the carrier that undercuts its rivals. Because there is little demand for last-minute seat availability, airlines flying leisure routes can operate with very high load factors. Availability of peak-time capacity is an important need for the leisure traveller. Airlines cater for the leisure market in two distinct ways. First, it is used to supplement high-yield business traffic. Every service will have a break-even load factor, so that any additional passengers will generate profit, even if it is low-yield. On short-haul services, low-yield leisure travellers, purchasing highly restricted tickets, which may not permit cancellation or booking alterations and require Saturday night stop-overs, will be given inferior cabin service, although they often occupy the same seats at an identical pitch to those travelling in business class. Many short-haul aircraft, especially narrow-bodies, lack separate cabins, the distinction being marked by mobile screens that can be moved along the aircraft fuselage in response to the relative demand for business and economy classes. On long-haul services, low-yield economy-class passengers again contribute to profit but will be given less seating space as well as an inferior cabin service to those in business classes. Long-haul aircraft are commonly configured into three classes—first, business and economy, although some operators have been combining the first two in order to maximise yields in a depressed market.

Secondly, leisure passengers can be carried by dedicated low-cost airlines. In Europe, the so-called 'charter' market has evolved into a completely deregulated and highly efficient industry, comprising a mixture of specialist airlines and subsidiaries of the large scheduled companies (Lyth and Dierikx, 1994). These carriers link European cities with resorts, particularly in the Mediterranean, but also, increasingly, throughout the world. The charter airlines tend to have modern, fuel-efficient fleets, often leased, the aircraft being used much more intensively than those operated by scheduled airlines. All IT operators compensate for low yield by seeking very high load factors and maximising aircraft seating capacity. For example, BA operates B767–300s at 247 or 193 seats on European and medium-haul routes respectively; one leisure carrier operates the same aircraft at 326 seats. Representative figures for the B757 are 180 seats on BA, compared to 235 on a UK leisure carrier.

In the past, the charter carriers served the traditional short-haul IT market for skiing and summer packages. Progressively, however, regulations have been liberalised, and most tour companies now also sell seat-only space on the aircraft for which they are contracted. Within the European Union (EU), the most recent set of aviation legislatory measures, implemented in January 1993, completed this process by abolishing the distinction between scheduled and chartered services (see Chapter 8). The intra-European short-haul IT market is probably close to saturation, even though disposable incomes are rising. The most notable recent trend in the package market has been the promotion of medium- and long-haul destinations in North America, Africa and Asia. Such leisure markets, however, represent alternative rather than additional destinations, income and time constraints ensuring that maximum travel demand in the leisure sector has probably been reached in Western Europe (Doganis, 1992a).

CARGO

The demand for air transport is also segmented between passengers and cargo, both often being combined on the same aircraft. About 75 per cent of air freight is carried on international services; approximately half the remaining domestic traffic is accounted for by the North American market (Doganis, 1991). Air cargo predominantly comprises high-value, low-bulk or low-weight commodities. Thus, it is common for a freight aircraft to 'bulk-out' before its payload limitation is reached. The market is segmented between emergency freight, high-value freight, routine perishables such as fruit, vegetables and flowers, and general cargo. The industry tends to be controlled by 'forwarders'—agents who buy space on the aircraft—rather than by the airlines themselves.

Three factors are currently responsible for influencing the demand and supply of cargo capacity. First, the air cargo market is extremely sensitive to recession and even minor fluctuations in world economic growth. Secondly, the introduction of wide-bodied jets changed the entire nature of the air freight business. These aircraft can carry substantial amounts of cargo in their belly-holds, using specially designed containers. The final factor concerns the emergence of the 'integrator' carrier, a firm handling large volumes of overnight packages for next-day delivery.

Recent patterns in the air cargo market reflect the interaction of these factors. The 1960s was an era of major economic growth in most advanced economies. The air cargo industry was dominated by European and North American carriers, largely using dedicated freighters. Substantial changes occurred during the 1970s as increasing numbers of wide-bodies markedly boosted available cargo capacity. A B747 with a full passenger load can still carry about 20 tons of cargo, compared to a payload of 60–70 tons for a pure freighter B747. Additionally, 'combi' aircraft carry both passengers and freight on the main deck. Moreover, Asian-Pacific carriers began to erode the dominant position of European and North American airlines. More markets were

Table 2.2. Top 10 freight carriers, 1993

Rank	Carrier	State	Scheduled freight tonnes carried (000s)
1	Lufthansa	Germany	737
2	FedEx	United States	557
3	Air France	France	549
4	Korean	South Korea	492
5	KLM	Netherlands	478
6	Singapore	Singapore	467
7	JAL	Japan	432
8	BA	United Kingdom	429
9	Cathay Pacific	Hong Kong	388
10	Northwest	United States	316

Source: IATA (1994).

served by non-scheduled flights operated by specialist charter cargo carriers, one means of circumventing restrictions placed on scheduled services by inter-governmental air service agreements (ASAs; see Chapter 3).

By the early 1980s, dedicated freighters accounted for around only 30 per cent of capacity, compared to about 70 per cent in 1969. Although the widespread deployment of wide-bodies, combined with a turbulent world economy, has since produced some over-supply of freight capacity, freighters now account for about 45 per cent of the market. This reflects the emergence of the intergrator carriers and reductions in cargo payloads on passenger aircraft caused by increases in passenger weight and the extra fuel required by the new-generation ultra-long-range aircraft. Excepting BA and FedEx, the latter purely a freight carrier, all the top cargo airlines employ dedicated cargo aircraft to supplement their passenger fleets (Table 2.2).

The airline response to the air cargo market follows one of two strategies. The world market remains dominated by European and Asian-Pacific carriers, Northwest being the only major US passenger-carrying airline among the top 10 freight carriers. To these airlines, cargo represents a considerable investment in facilities, aircraft, marketing and higher-yield branded services. Despite these capital requirements, cargo can make a substantial contribution to airline profits, while freight revenue can be used to supplement that from passengers in opening up new routes. Conversely, many carriers, including some of the largest, adopt no more than an opportunist attitude to air cargo. In such cases freight is carried on passenger aircraft and, because of the absence of dedicated tailored services, is relatively low yield.

Undoubtedly, the most significant recent development in air cargo has been the rise of the integrated overnight package airline, typified by FedEx, a development made possible by the US Air Cargo Deregulation Act of 1978. Integrators tap demand from complex inter-connected economies, exploiting computer technology to function efficiently (Kuby and Gray, 1993). They focus on an airport hub, which does not, in itself, have to be a significant market; the primary requirement is sufficient night-time runway capacity. The incoming aircraft at FedEx's Memphis hub arrive between 10.30pm and 1.30am; packages are then sorted and the aircraft depart between 3.00 and 5.00am. Road transport is used for door-to-door pick-up and delivery. All the market entrants in the overnight package business have established networks on the FedEx model (R. Hall, 1989).

The scale of these operations is underlined by the size of the largest companies involved. FedEx employs 110 000 people and has a fleet of over 200 jet aircraft of B727 size and above, plus some 250 small feeder planes. United Parcel Service (UPS), which specialises in world-wide package delivery, operates around 160 large jet aircraft and employs 300 000 people. Following similar principles, albeit on a much smaller scale, some national post offices operate overnight mail delivery networks. In the United Kingdom, for example, the Royal Mail's Skynet employs 10 airlines to operate routes centred on Liverpool and East Midlands airports.

SOCIO-ECONOMIC DETERMINANTS OF CONSUMER BEHAVIOUR IN AIR TRANSPORT

As the preceding discussion has indicated, the primary determinant of consumer behaviour in air transport may be the dichotomy between travellers who are paying for journeys with their own earned income and those who are not. Given this basic segmentation, demand for air transport—expressed as the propensity to fly—is strongly related to occupation and income. Other socio-demographic characteristics, including gender and age-structure, are also significant factors as are geographical disparities in development. Although a majority among populations of developed countries possess the financial resources to travel by air, variations in regional income still cause differential patterning in demand.

OCCUPATION AND INCOME

Some of the most detailed statistics on the socio-economic characteristics of airline passengers, available in the public domain, are contained in various passenger surveys conducted by the UK Civil Aviation Authority (CAA). Table 2.3 shows the extent of air travel by socio-economic group (SEG) for a selection of airports surveyed by the CAA between 1991–3. Unsurprisingly, the data confirm that occupation and income are the primary determinants of the propensity to travel by air. This replicates the situation in the United States, where there is a clear correlation between high income and most travelled by air and low income and least travelled. In the United Kingdom,

Table 2.3. Business and leisure air travel by socio-economic groups (SEG*) for selected UK airports, 1991–3 (percentage of total passengers at each airport)

Airport	Business SEGs				Leisure SEGs				Total SEGs			
	A/B	C1	C2	D/E	A/B	C1	C2	D/E	A/B	C1	C2	D/E
Heathrow	66.7	27.4	5.2	0.7	42.2	36.1	12.8	8.9	56.1	31.1	8.5	4.3
Gatwick	59.5	33.9	5.5	1.1	37.1	39.0	14.9	9.0	41.9	37.9	12.9	7.3
Birmingham	43.6	49.3	6.0	1.2	23.1	41.3	18.0	17.5	28.5	43.4	14.9	13.3
East Midlands	42.4	48.4	7.9	1.3	19.8	40.5	21.8	17.9	23.5	41.8	19.5	15.1
Leeds/Bradford	65.6	26.0	6.4	2.0	34.8	26.5	20.5	18.3	47.5	26.3	14.6	11.5
Manchester	60.6	33.0	5.1	1.2	24.9	34.4	25.6	15.2	30.5	34.2	22.4	13.0
UK Population 1992	25.9	21.0	30.3	22.8	25.9	21.0	30.3	22.8	25.9	21.0	30.3	22.8

* A/B—Professional and managerial; C1—intermediate non-manual; C2—skilled manual; D—semi-skilled and unskilled; E—residual (unemployed, pensioners etc.)

Sources: CAA (1993a and b).

those employed in professional, managerial and intermediate non-manual occupations (SEGs A/B and C1) are most likely to travel by air for both business and leisure reasons. Conversely, skilled, semi-skilled and unskilled manual workers (SEGs C2 and D), together with the residual E category, are significantly under-represented in relation to their proportion of the population as a whole. In 1991–3, the average income of UK international business travellers ranged from £34 000 at Leeds/Bradford to £55 000 at Heathrow; the average across the six airports shown in Table 2.3 was £40 000.

More people travel for leisure than for business purposes. In the UK sample, the proportion of business travellers ranges from only 14 per cent at London Gatwick to 60 per cent on London Heathrow domestic flights (Table 2.4). The business market has also been undergoing a fundamental change. Given the speed advantages and, moreover, the fall in real costs of air travel, more junior staff have begun travelling on business as trade and industry

Table 2.4. Journey purpose at selected UK airports, 1991–3

Airport	Percentage business travellers	Percentage leisure travellers
Heathrow (domestic)	60	40
Heathrow (international)	40	60
Gatwick	14	86
Birmingham	33	67
East Midlands	20	80
Leeds/Bradford	45	55
Manchester	20	80

Sources: CAA (1993a and b).

Table 2.5. Employment sectors of business passengers at selected UK airports, 1992–3 (percentage of total business passengers at each airport)

Airport	Banking and finance	Public services	Metal goods and engineering	Total for three sectors
Heathrow	23.8	19.8	16.2	59.8
Gatwick	22.6	21.7	13.5	57.8
Birmingham	15.8	14.5	24.5	54.8
East Midlands	11.8	16.5	20.2	48.5
Leeds/Bradford	19.9	17.5	15.9	53.3
Manchester	15.0	16.6	16.6	48.2
Average	18.2	17.8	17.8	53.8
UK average as main business	12.1	32.5	9.3	

Sources: CAA (1993a and b).

becomes more internationalised. This is one factor accounting for the substantial presence of intermediate non-manual workers (SEG C1) among business travellers (Doganis, 1991).

The data in Table 2.3 also demonstrate that significant regional variations occur in the class composition of business air travellers, even within a small country like the United Kingdom; in turn, these reflect variations in the geographical distribution of the principal business sectors. Three economic activities—banking and finance, public services and metal goods/engineering—account for between 48 and 60 per cent of all business travel (Table 2.5). As manufacturing declines, banking/finance and public services are the two most rapidly growing sectors in the UK economy, although the distribution and catering sector ranks second after public services in terms of employment. It is significantly under-represented, however, in terms of air travel. Although declining, metal goods and engineering is still the pre-eminent UK manufacturing sector. Both Birmingham and East Midlands airports, those where intermediate non-manual is the principal business SEG, serve areas in which its importance remains most marked. Conversely, the two airports with the highest percentages of professional and managerial travellers—Heathrow and Leeds/Bradford—have an above-average representation of banking and finance passengers.

Although the banking/finance and public-service sectors are more important in absolute terms in generating air traffic, relative demand is considerably greater among those employed in the production industries (Table 2.6). Maximum propensity to fly is actually found among employees of businesses in extraction processes, energy and water supply and metal/engineering industries, particularly if they live outside the South-east region. Conversely, those employed in the tertiary sector are much less likely

Table 2.6. Propensity to travel by air by employment sector, 1992–3*

Employment sector	Central England airports[1] (all business passengers)	London area airports[2] (UK business passenger only)
Agriculture	0.3	0.38
Energy/water supply	2.79	2.84
Extraction processes	3.62	2.07
Metal goods/engineering	2.28	1.69
Other manufacturing	1.33	0.97
Total productive industries	2.03	1.50
Construction	0.77	0.90
Distribution/catering	0.51	0.37
Transport/communications	1.33	1.43
Banking/finance	1.12	1.97
Public services	0.47	0.61
Total tertiary sector	0.66	1.19

* Business sector percentage of all business passengers, divided by percentage in UK working population as whole.
[1] Birmingham, East Midlands, Leeds/Bradford, Manchester.
[2] Heathrow, Gatwick, City, Luton, Stansted.

Sources: CAA (1993a and b).

to fly, although banking/finance accounts for more air travel in South-east England than it does in the Midlands. As productive industries continue to decline, these trends in propensity to travel by air are important in predicting future demand for services from UK regional airports. In particular, continued growth in demand for UK business air travel depends on the employment sectors that demonstrate lower propensities to fly.

The distribution of leisure passengers by SEG is likely to be rather more representative of the population as a whole than is true for business traffic (Table 2.3). None the less, A/Bs and C1s are again over-represented, while C2s and D/Es remain under-represented in relation to their proportions within the population as a whole. Thus, between 60 and 80 per cent of leisure traffic is generated by the A/B and C1 SEGs, although these account for only 47 per cent of the UK population. The CAA surveys show that the proportions of passengers from the lower SEGs declined during the late 1980s and early 1990s, indicating the effects of recession on the less affluent, particularly their inability to purchase IT holidays. Disposable household income is the most significant variable influencing the demand for leisure travel. The lowest percentages of leisure travellers for the C2, D and E SEGs were recorded at Heathrow and Gatwick, reflecting their location within the United Kingdom's highest cost region.

AGE AND GENDER

The propensity to travel by air can also be differentiated by age and gender. Again, there are significant variations between business and leisure travellers, more so for gender than for age. The average age of both business and leisure passengers surveyed at UK airports remains constant at around 38–40, reflecting the age structure of the population as a whole. The peak is less marked for leisure passengers, who include significant numbers of children and elderly. Recent surveys have shown that the economic recession of the early 1990s depressed demand for leisure travel from households with children more than those without; a substantial majority of leisure travellers have no children aged under 16 living in the household.

The business and leisure markets display markedly dissimilar gender mixes. Most recent surveys indicate an increase in the percentage of women travelling for business purposes, although, at most airports, women still account for no more than 15 per cent of this market. Conversely, they comprise between 50 and 55 per cent of leisure travellers. In the United States, women also generate over half of all trips in the leisure market.

GEOGRAPHICAL DISPARITIES IN DEVELOPMENT

Inevitably, if income is the primary determinant of both business and leisure air travel, national and regional variations in wealth will influence the pattern of demand. The world's wealthiest countries account for most scheduled passenger traffic; global disparities are discussed in more detail in Chapter 5. At the national scale, the propensity of the UK population to travel by air is markedly differentiated by regional economic performance (Figure 2.3). At the aggregate level, the South-east is the only UK planning region to score a ratio greater than 1:1, when the volume of international passengers generated per planning region is compared to the populations of those regions. Indeed, it generates around twice as many trips per head of population as do any other planning regions. Although this is partly due to the major international airports, Heathrow and Gatwick, attracting passengers from elsewhere in the United Kingdom, the superiority of the South-east in this respect also reflects its dominant position within the UK economy. Again, the largest growth in both business and leisure traffic (except IT) is occurring in East Anglia. In part, this can be attributed to the development of Stansted as a third London airport but is also due to the pre-eminence of East Anglia, among all the UK regions, in virtually every index of prosperity from employment and consumer spending to quality of life. Conversely, Wales and the North of England, the two regions that display the least aggregate propensity to fly, are among the most depressed in the country. Wales is a declining heavy industrial, peripheral region; its economy under-performs that of the United Kingdom generally. The North of

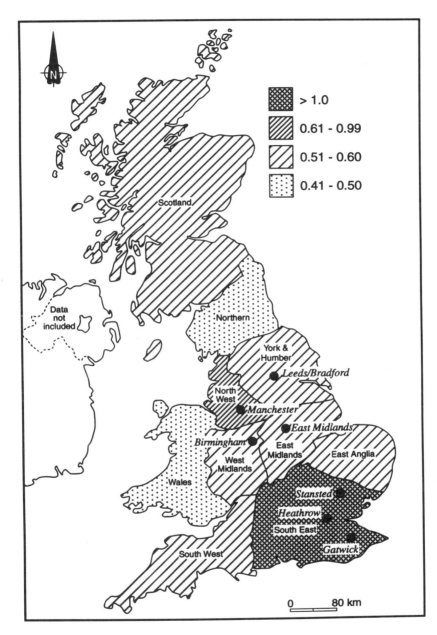

Figure 2.3. Propensity to fly by planning region for UK international passengers, 1991 (measured by dividing international passengers per planning region by population total per planning region)
Source: CAA, 1993b

England is a region of declining employment, weak growth and low consumer demand.

However, the relationship between regional economic performance and propensity for air travel is complicated by spatial variations between the business and leisure sectors. In terms of IT flights, the highest propensity to fly actually occurs in the North-west and North of England planning regions, while, conversely, ratios for the South-east, South-west and East Anglia regions have dropped significantly. Although this trend may reflect regional variations in SEG distributions—in particular that of skilled manual workers who constitute the most common class among leisure travellers at most UK airports—it is also related to spatial variations in disposable income. Thus, southern and eastern England may have comparatively high salaries and low unemployment, but housing and congestion costs are high. Conversely, the North-west region faces growing unemployment, increasing out-migration and poor output growth, but, to date, disposable incomes have remained relatively high for those employed, particularly because of lower housing costs. The decline in the IT market in the South-east, South-west and East Anglia regions may also reflect changing fashions in holiday destinations.

AIRLINES AND CONSUMER BEHAVIOUR

While the propensity to fly will be governed by the socio-economic circumstances of individuals and regions, once consumers enter the air transport market their behaviour is also conditioned by the marketing activities of airlines. The airline that carries the largest share of traffic, originating at an airport, will be able to attract a disproportionate share of traffic on any particular route emanating from that airport. This characteristic appears to be attributable to marketing strength and to supplier strategies that manipulate consumer behaviour and encourage brand loyalty (Borenstein, 1991). The literature identifies two particular strategies. First, it has been argued that the development of sophisticated Computer Reservation Systems (CRSs) confer major competitive advantages to their airline owners because they can be used to manipulate consumer behaviour. Secondly, Frequent Flyer Programmes (FFPs) and Travel Agent Commission Overrides (TACOs) are used to induce brand loyalty.

Because the data held on CRSs are the principal source of information concerning consumer behaviour, much concern has been expressed that these systems are inherently anti-competitive. Requiring very large investment, there are only a handful of such systems world-wide, mostly owned by alliances of the largest carriers (Figure 2.4). Studies in the United States have shown that travel agents tend to book around 50 per cent of their sales from the first screen showing; further, they are likely to be tied to one CRS system, these tending to have geographical monopolies around the major airports served by their owner airlines. For example, 80 per cent of automated UK travel agents use *Galileo*, part-owned by BA; on several occasions, the carrier has been accused of using this privileged access to mount predatory actions against competing airlines.

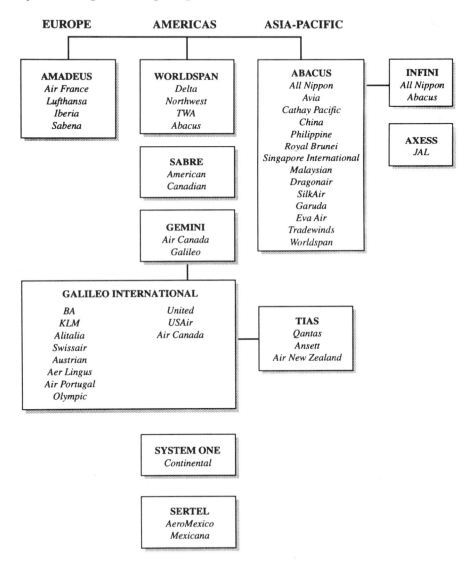

Figure 2.4. CRS industry global structure, 1994
Based on Humphreys, 1994; WTO, 1994

However, it is now argued that the direct anti-competitive advantages of CRS ownership are less important than might once have been the case. One study of dominant airline behaviour found the effects of CRS bias to be small and difficult to distinguish statistically (Borenstein, 1991). There are a number of reasons for this, including regulation which has eliminated the more blatant forms of CRS bias (Humphreys, 1990; Truitt et al., 1991). In Europe, for example, every airline, irrespective of size, now has the right to have its services distributed fairly in each CRS market. Further, globalisation of CRS provision, and the enormous capital investment required by this technology, means that possibly only three core systems will survive. Therefore, access to CRSs, as straightforward reservation systems, is considerably less privileged than it was in the past, and smaller carriers have probably less to fear from the so-called 'hosting' benefits which might once have accrued to the large owner airlines.

Nevertheless, in one crucial respect, major carriers still derive important advantages from CRSs. These systems are the primary sources of the immensely sophisticated market intelligence required to operate efficient yield-management programmes. Theoretically, any airline can access this data, but, in reality, only the largest have sufficient capital resources to buy it, together with the computer capacity necessary to use the information effectively (Humphreys, 1994). The intelligence gained from CRSs enables such airlines to target segmented markets and sub-markets much more effectively than their competitors and to gauge consumer response to fares initiatives and promotions. In addition, CRSs also provide market intelligence on competitive carriers, forced to use the system through lack of alternatives.

Secondly, airlines have invested heavily in developing FFPs, which, essentially, are a form of loyalty payment. American Airlines' Advantage Program, the first scheme of its kind, proved such a successful marketing device that most of the world's major airlines have since been forced to follow suit. Largely aimed at business passengers who may have no incentive to economise on the cost of air travel, FFPs award points that can be converted into free travel. The amount credited per flight or transaction is pegged to distance travelled and amount spent (Humphreys, 1991). In many cases, airlines have formed FFP alliances among themselves, and with car-hire and hotel chains. Consumer surveys have found that first and business class passengers rate an airline's FFP almost as important a priority as punctuality and on-board comfort. High service standards are no longer sufficient to retain consumer loyalty and virtually every airline with substantial business traffic is now obliged to offer an FFP.

Humphreys (1991) identifies three reasons why these programmes constitute a method of manipulating consumer behaviour, particularly for large carriers. Firstly, travellers may trade-up to higher fare levels, which generate more FFP points, particularly as the schemes are aimed at the business market in which the employer or client is paying the fare. FFPs offer their

business membe
carriers with ext
wide range of desi
are part of a brand .
not only to aircraft .
ins and additional ex
FFP points. Thirdly, t.
providing airlines wit\
able and frequent passe
ascertain the effects of T.
These schemes work in \
bonuses accrue to travel .
steering passengers to pai
those carriers offer the best .

GEOGRAP

Volume of
air transport
market

THE FORECASTING OF F

At the global scale, the pattern of   ∪₁y fixed by
an inertia attributable to the pre   ∪₁ major cities and
economic activity, while the aggre   .ıor air transport is strongly
related to trends in economic grow   . uecline. Thus, there is a fair corre-
spondence between Gross Domestic Product (GDP) and Revenue Passenger
Kms (RPKs) flown. The RPK/GDP ratio once stood at 2:1 but is now declining. It is estimated that a three per cent increase in GDP is now worth only a
four per cent increase in air traffic, a function of the increasing maturity of
the market. Nevertheless, because of this relationship, air transport is extremely vulnerable to recession or even less dramatic economic downturns.
A prolonged recession in the United States was partly responsible for US
carriers losing $5.8 billion in 1990–1, an amount estimated to have consumed
all the profits made by the industry since the first flight of the Wright
Brothers in 1903 (Dempsey and Goetz, 1992). Admittedly, the extent of these
losses was magnified by world political events, over-capacity and excessive
debt servicing, but this illustrates the vulnerability of the industry to external economic and political factors.

Concepts such as maturity and saturation depend upon the assumption
that an air transport market corresponds to the product life-cycle concept
used in marketing (Figure 2.5). Saturation occurs when the demand for a
good or service is not expected to increase; maturity implies a slowing down
in growth of demand for a product as the market approaches saturation (A.
Graham, 1993). It is likely that some airline markets, especially in North
America and Europe, are approaching this condition. In the US domestic
market, for example, airline passenger revenue as a percentage of both GDP
and personal consumption has remained relatively constant since 1980.

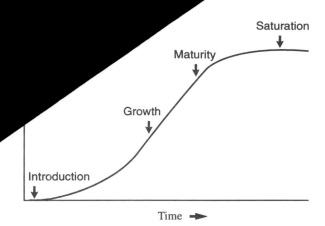

Figure 2.5. Air transport demand in a particular market over time
Based on A. Graham, 1993

Again due to the relationship between income and the propensity for air travel, the maximum potential market, even in the wealthiest countries, is unlikely to exceed around 80 per cent of the population. Thus, the proportion of the US population that has ever flown has now levelled out at around 75 per cent. Again, UK passenger surveys reveal very low numbers of first-time flyers—around one in 100 and three to five in 100 for business and leisure markets, respectively. For additional trips, saturation can occur because of time and income constraints. Thus, higher incomes do not necessarily generate more leisure journeys.

Economic growth and market saturation are not the only factors accounting for the vulnerability of the air transport industry to external forces, thereby causing deviations from the S-shaped demand curve. For example, the Gulf War of 1991 dramatically depressed an international scheduled air transport market already softened by economic recession in North America and Europe. Premium traffic was particularly badly hit, 1991 becoming the worst year in aviation financial history as demand dropped by 33 per cent. In total, IATA carriers accumulated losses of no less than $11.5 billion between 1990–3. Self-inflicted problems, including low yields, over-capacity and high costs, also contributed to the magnitude of these losses.

The potential demand for air transport is also affected by competition from other modes of transport and from telecommunications. In Europe and Japan, this means rail as well as road networks. For example, the European Commission (EC) is promoting the development of a trans-European high-speed train (HST) network (see Chapter 14). Although slower than aircraft, HSTs are competitive on city-centre to city-centre times over distances of up to 500 kms. The inauguration of France's first *Train à Grande Vitesse* (*TGV*) line between Paris and Lyon in 1981 halved domestic air traffic between the two cities. The *TGV-Nord* between Paris and Lille, opened in 1993, will eventually offer onward HST connections into Belgium, the Netherlands and Germany. It also serves the Channel Tunnel, which opened to passenger services in late 1994 (Gibb, ed., 1994). It is predicted that this inter-modal competition will lead to a serious erosion of the airlines' share of the London–Paris and London–Brussels markets; the former is the world's busiest international airline city-pairing, catering for over three million passengers per annum. Although estimates vary, it has been calculated that, by 2000, Eurotunnel will have cost the airlines a total of around three million passengers per year.

It is also likely that further developments in telecommunications, particularly video-conferencing, will depress business demand for air transport. Again, studies have arrived at different conclusions, but it has been estimated that up to 25 per cent of business travel could be eliminated through high-technology substitution by 2010. Recession has made companies more aware of the costs of corporate travel, although surveys have shown that senior executives, who incur the highest travel costs, are least likely to have their business journeys eliminated by video-conferencing. This suggests that premium high-yield traffic should be less affected by technological advances than economy class (*Airline Business*, November, 1994). It also intimates that business travel may often be as much a 'perk' as a necessity. Combining inter-modal and telecommunications competition, BAA (formerly British Airports Authority) estimates that airlines serving Heathrow could face a 10 per cent loss in business traffic by 2010, equivalent to about seven million passengers per year.

Another major imponderable affecting future demand for air transport is the cost of fuel. In the past, changes in fuel price have had important effects on airline costs and traffic, particularly during the 1970s with the escalation in costs that followed the oil embargo organised by the Organisation of Petroleum Exporting Countries (OPEC). Fuel accounts for about 25 per cent of airline industry costs. Although there were some fluctuations in price associated with the Gulf War, fuel prices have remained relatively stable, having little recent impact on yields and traffic. All fuel is priced in US dollars, however, which means that non-US carriers are exposed to fluctuations in foreign-currency exchange markets.

Future passenger demand is also a function of demographic change and the global distribution of economic growth. North American and European markets are largely mature or approaching saturation, the current potential for real growth in air transport being in some Asian-Pacific countries. Some of these states have large populations and increasingly buoyant economies. Most notably, China, which accounts for 25 per cent of the global population, is emerging as a major civil aviation market both in its own right and as a tourist destination. For example, it is now Boeing's single most

Table 2.7. Scheduled passenger traffic forecast for 1995 (passenger-km performed)

Region	Forecast growth in GDP (%)	Forecast passengers (millions)	Forecast growth (%)
Africa	3.5	52 700	6.5
Asia-Pacific	5.8	543 800	10.6
Europe	2.0	617 500	4.7
Middle East	8.5	64 500	6.8
North America	2.8	978 800	7.0
Latin America/Caribbean	3.2	110 900	7.9
World	2.8	2 368 200	7.3

Source: ICAO (1993, p.29).

important region for new-aircraft sales, a crucial reason behind the Clinton administration's 1994 renewal of China's 'most-favoured nation' status, despite widespread concerns over the country's civil rights record.

Forecasts of future passenger demand largely originate from interested parties, particularly ICAO and the three major aircraft manufacturers. They all agree that Asia-Pacific is the market likely to experience the most significant growth in air transport demand throughout the remainder of the 1990s. ICAO predicts an annual increase in GDP in Asian-Pacific countries in excess of five per cent per annum for the remainder of this decade, compared to figures of between three and four per cent in North America, and only two per cent or less in Europe. The Middle East is the only region expected to exceed the Asia-Pacific region in terms of GDP growth. While this is an important regional air transport market, it is also a relatively minor one in the global context, limited as it is by a small demographic base. On the basis of passenger kms performed, ICAO forecasts a growth in excess of 10 per cent for the Asia-Pacific region by 1995, compared to 4.7 and 7.0 per cent in Europe and North America respectively, and a world average of 7.3 per cent (Table 2.7). European growth is depressed by slow economic recovery and the inclusion of Eastern Europe and the CIS. At present, this latter market is too volatile to predict with any great hope of accuracy. Elsewhere, the relatively optimistic growth rates envisaged are predicated upon an improved world-economy.

CONCLUSIONS

Demand for air transport is a rather more complex issue than might first be anticipated. As the foregoing discussion has indicated, the lack of behavioural research, particularly into consumer response to supplier-led marketing strategies, creates a major lacuna in our understanding of demand.

Given that difficulty, the relationship between GDP, disposable income and propensity to fly essentially constrains the markets open to air transport, a factor of real significance in discussing patterns of competition within the industry. Furthermore, the supply of air transport is a function not of demand alone but also of the political forces to which the industry is subject, the economic characteristics of air transport itself and the increasing globalisation of the world-economy. These factors are discussed in the subsequent chapters in Part One.

3   The Geopolitics of Air Transport

The geography of air transport is inseparable from the domain of national self-interest and political advantage. To varying degrees, airlines do operate under market conditions of profit and loss, but their activities remain controlled and regulated by underlying political constraints and policies. The most salient changes during the past several decades have been concerned with the introduction of competition and deregulation—or liberalisation—throughout much of the world's airline industry. This can be seen as part of a much wider general onslaught against the oligopolistic control of transport markets by a very small number of suppliers (Button, 1991; Knowles and Hall, 1992).

This chapter discusses some of the prominent aspects of aeropolitics, many of the general points raised being pursued in Part Two where the geographies of air transport throughout the world's regions are discussed.

Broadly, the topics considered can be divided into four categories:

(i)   the relationships between air transport and inter-governmental agreements;
(ii) commitments to, and policies for, competition, deregulation (or liberalisation) and privatisation;
(iii) the relationships between the air transport industry and the specialist government agencies responsible for its administration;
(iv) the role of air transport within broader economic and social policies.

Unavoidably, political policies for air transport depend upon the wider priorities of governments and, moreover, reflect their ideological orientations. Consequently, air transport policy is characterised by numerous conflicts of interest involving governments, their regulatory agencies, airlines and consumers.

AIR TRANSPORT AND INTER-GOVERNMENTAL AGREEMENTS

Once it was accepted in the Paris Convention of 1919 that states possess sovereign rights to the air space above their territories, direct government intervention into air transport became inevitable (Doganis, 1991). As airlines developed during the 1920s and 1930s, they were used as instruments of state policy to promote trade, mail services, aerospace industries, foreign political linkages and domestic employment, all without much regard to economic implications or commercial significance. Air transport networks developed on the basis of national need, airlines becoming part of the very symbolic iconography of the state's identity, their logos often stylised representations of national emblems. British Airways, for example, may be a private company, owned by an array of investors, many of whom are foreign, but, through its corporate imagery, it still claims to represent Britain.

Governments generally regard their national airlines—even privatised ones—as flag-carrying representations of national interest, one reason used to justify continued state protection of those airlines. Civil carriers may also be allocated a strategic role in national defence policies, one example being the United States Civil Reserve Air Fleet, somewhat modified airliners that can be re-called from revenue service if demands of national security so dictate. Furthermore, aviation in its broadest sense is a major employer. In the United States, about 1.5 million people are employed in high-skill, high-wage jobs in the airline and aerospace industries. Aerospace is the country's largest manufacturing export sector, while tourism, which depends directly on air transport, employs eight per cent of the total working population and contributes over six per cent of GNP. The airports serving the 30 largest metropolitan areas generate more than $250 billion in economic activity, $80 billion in wages and four million direct and indirect jobs (National Commission, 1993).

Inevitably, therefore, strong airline and aerospace industries are in the national interest, a factor fundamental to the politics of international air transport. Airlines do not fly international routes solely in response to commercial criteria of profit, loss and market demand. The provision of international air services is conditional upon the constraints of some 2000 intergovernmental bilateral ASAs, involving 160 countries, all of which reflect political as well as commercial priorities (Findlay and Forsyth, 1992). The international politics of contemporary air transport date from the Chicago Convention of 1944 and the establishment of ICAO in 1947. The central principles of the Convention established that air services should be provided 'on the basis of equality of opportunity and operated soundly and economically'. It recognised the so-called 'five freedoms of civil aviation' (to which three more have since been added) (Figure 3.1; Sealy, 1966; Shearman, 1992; Association of European Airlines—AEA, 1993). The multilateral exploitation of these freedoms was rejected, however, the Chicago Convention agreeing only to the mutual exchange of the first two: the right to overfly a foreign country and the right to make a non-traffic generating stop, for example, to refuel. Even then, not all countries—most notably the former USSR—accepted these. All other freedoms were left to ASAs, negotiated between governments.

The basic principle of all bilaterals is reciprocity or equivalency, defined as the equal and fair exchange of aviation rights (Debbage, 1994). Issues

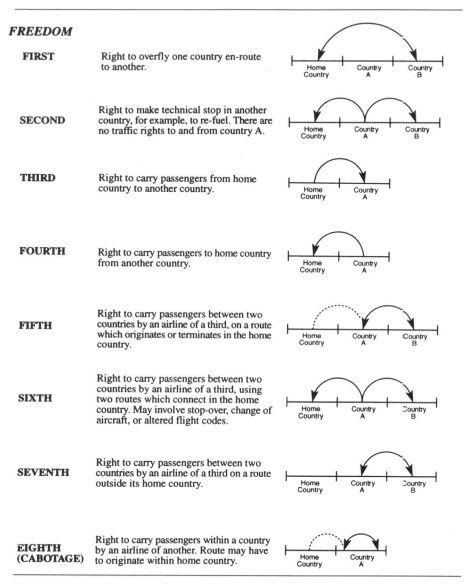

FREEDOM

FIRST — Right to overfly one country en-route to another.

SECOND — Right to make technical stop in another country, for example, to re-fuel. There are no traffic rights to and from country A.

THIRD — Right to carry passengers from home country to another country.

FOURTH — Right to carry passengers to home country from another country.

FIFTH — Right to carry passengers between two countries by an airline of a third, on a route which originates or terminates in the home country.

SIXTH — Right to carry passengers between two countries by an airline of a third, using two routes which connect in the home country. May involve stop-over, change of aircraft, or altered flight codes.

SEVENTH — Right to carry passengers between two countries by an airline of a third on a route outside its home country.

EIGHTH (CABOTAGE) — Right to carry passengers within a country by an airline of another. Route may have to originate within home country.

Figure 3.1.   Air freedom rights
Sources: AEA Yearbook, 1993; Shearman, 1992

covered include fares, tariffs, capacity, frequency, number of carriers and routes flown. The actual airlines selected to operate the services specified in bilaterals are generally nominated later by their respective governments. Initially, ASAs were highly protectionist: restricting capacity, requiring double governmental approval of fares and nominating only one airline per route from each state, both operating identical tariff structures. Such agreements also permitted pooling arrangements, allocating equitable shares of revenue generated to those two carriers. There was little, if any, provision for fifth-freedom rights (the right to carry passengers between two foreign countries). Protectionist ASAs, now less common than in the past, are clearly anti-competitive in that they pre-empt any possibility of market entry by potential competitors to the government-sanctioned duopoly (Doganis, 1991).

The 1946 US–UK Bermuda accord on North Atlantic air services acted as the model for a more liberal form of bilateral. While accepting fare controls, it permitted fifth-freedom rights, although the total capacity offered by the airlines operating these sectors had to be related to the end-to-end capacity of the route. However, the grievance procedure, designed to safeguard against the abuse of capacity levels, could be invoked only after the event (MacKenzie, 1991; Dierikx, 1992). Where possible, Bermuda-type agreements, which do not preclude pooling, have left the co-ordination of tariff structures to IATA. Amongst other liberalising conditions, the 1977 re-negotiation of the US–UK bilateral—Bermuda 2—allowed limited multiple designation of carriers on transatlantic services. Some ASAs permit multiple designation on city-pairs; others restrict it to country-pairs, meaning that a specific route is still served by only two airlines. Bermuda 2 contained provision for both circumstances, although multiple designation of carriers on city-pairs has been restricted to only four routes.

The original Bermuda accord on the North Atlantic, and subsequent US bilaterals with Asian states, were agreed between unequal partners, a reflection of the political dominance of the United States and the ability of its airlines to operate services in the aftermath of World War II. The grand construction of US global hegemony occurred in these years, rooted in the political institutions that it built to oppose Communism and promote free trade (Wallerstein, 1991). The US attitude to bilaterals must be placed within this ideological context, as should the contemporary conflict created by these agreements, particularly in Asia-Pacific (see Chapter 11). Wallerstein argues that the United States has subsequently sought to slow down the consequences of its economic decline, by utilising the institutions of its hegemonic control of the world-economy. The aggressive pursuit of fifth-freedom, or beyond, air rights into Asia-Pacific and Europe in post-war bilaterals, still confers major and unreciprocated contemporary commercial advantages upon US carriers operating in these markets.

For example, the 1952 bilateral agreement between the United States and Japan gave the former virtually unrestricted access to Tokyo and beyond and provides the basis for extensive contemporary US penetration into the intra-Asia-Pacific market. Such rights allow 'starburst' operations, particularly at Tokyo, where passengers connect from US-originating flights to others serving a multiplicity of destinations. In some bilaterals, this process can involve break-of-gauge rights, the substitution of smaller aircraft for the beyond sectors. Reciprocal access by Asian-Pacific or European carriers to US domestic markets would not count as fifth-freedom rights but as cabotage, which still remains illegal under US law. Some bilaterals do, however, specify fifth-freedom rights beyond the United States for both Asian-Pacific and European carriers.

The liberalised air transport regime of the past two decades has produced more flexible bilaterals, including those negotiated between various European countries during the 1980s (Abbott and Thompson, 1989). These agreements, such as those concluded by the United Kingdom with the Netherlands and Ireland, typically permitted open route access and multiple designation of carriers on country-pairs, and sometimes on city-pairs, while precluding capacity controls. Double approval of fares was replaced by double disapproval, the system whereby a tariff can be refused only if both governments reject it. Furthermore, pooling of revenue on routes is no longer permitted under EC rules.

Bermuda 2 was an example that the United States was keen not to follow and, since the onset of domestic deregulation in 1978, it has negotiated a series of more liberalised bilaterals, which have sought to set fares and services consistent with consumer demand, establish permissive route authorities and multiple designation (especially on country-pairs) eliminate capacity and frequency controls and increase the number of non-stop gateway cities (Boberg and Collison, 1989). The strategy has been to penetrate both North Atlantic and Pacific markets with 'beach-head' agreements, designed to force more recalcitrant governments into renegotiating their ASAs. The key accords were those with the Netherlands (1978) and Singapore (1979). Both were very liberal, granting improved access to the US market in return for fifth-freedom rights for US carriers (Debbage, 1994). Once such agreements are in place, other countries can be threatened with traffic diversion, although simultaneously offered the bait of increased access to the world's largest aviation market (Kasper, 1988). Currently, a number of states, most notably Japan, France and the United Kingdom, are actively resisting US pressures.

Most recently, the United States has offered to negotiate 'open-skies' bilaterals, allowing unrestricted market entry and code-sharing alliances (in which one service is operated under the flight codes of two airlines). Further, these agreements place no restrictions on intermediate points served and include double disapproval of fares. An accord, embracing these principles, was signed with the Netherlands in 1992, subsequently acting as the model for similar open-skies agreements offered to nine other small European countries (see Chapter 10). Thus, the US position is moving towards the conclusion that the bilateral system is no longer sound. It is insufficiently growth-oriented in a global trading environment. Bilaterals may allow foreign carriers unbalanced access to the US domestic market because no other state has a similarly-sized market to offer in return. That explains the tenacity with which the United States seeks and protects beyond rights (National Commission, 1993).

The logical outcome of this argument is the replacement of bilaterals with multilateral agreements, in which groups of like-minded countries permit any airline virtually unlimited access to any market within their boundaries. It can be argued that bilaterals cannot accommodate a fair and equal exchange of aviation rights because geography confers advantages on those few countries with an abundance of land and substantial domestic markets (Debbage, 1994). Indeed, the United States openly admits that its own agenda is best served by more liberal or open-skies ASAs—such as that concluded with Canada in February 1995—and trends towards global multilateralism. Post-deregulation US carriers have relatively low costs, the world's largest domestic market and numerous domestic gateways. Consequently, although US arguments call for the rigours of the open market to determine market share, this stance has aroused widespread cynicism, particularly given the continued protection of the US domestic market from foreign carriers. It is probably safe to assume that, whatever the rhetoric, all ASAs have been, and always will be, negotiated to maximise national interests (Lobbenberg, 1994). As air transport is a service industry, it could be made subject to multilateral trade agreements, conceivably under the General Agreement on Tariffs and Trade (GATT) (Henaku, 1993). The US government was instrumental in the Uruguay Round of negotiations to liberalise world trade in goods; along with other services, air transport is excluded from this agreement, but the possibility does exist that sometime in the future a multilateral framework for service industries may yet emerge (Daniels, 1993).

Consequently, despite the pro-competition ethos of the last two decades, international air transport remains a business conducted within absolute constraints of inter-governmental agreements. Inevitably, conflicts of interest ensue from this process. First, like all capitalistic enterprises, airlines are concerned with the suppression of competition and the establishment of actual or quasi-monopolies in their markets. These aims may conflict, however, with governmental commitments to competition in the interests of consumer choice, a policy likely to entail multiple designation of a country's carriers on country- and city-pairs. Secondly, although supposedly negotiated in the national interest, the specific terms of bilaterals are often influenced by the agendas of the dominant airlines. Route authorities and even airport runway slots, state assets negotiated in the public domain and supposedly in the public interest, are subsequently transferred to these, frequently private-sector, firms. As successful commercial exploitation of the opportunities offered by bilaterals requires investment, airlines tend to regard such rights as their own properties rather than, as it were, loans. Thus, in 1991, BA was incensed when some UK slots at Tokyo Narita were transferred to Virgin Atlantic (Virgin). The Secretary of State for Transport replied to BA's complaints: 'no airline has a legal right to a landing or take-off slot. Rather, airlines have permission and this must be subject to the public interest' (quoted in Gregory, 1994, p. 147).

POLICIES FOR COMPETITION, DEREGULATION, LIBERALISATION AND PRIVATISATION

Prior to 1978, when the passing of the US Airline Deregulation Act can be seen as the symbolic breakpoint with previous regulatory structures, airline activities world-wide were subject to strict control by government agencies such as the Civil Aeronautics Board (CAB) in the United States and the CAA in the United Kingdom. Airlines had to apply for licences to operate both international and domestic services, while tariff structures were subject to regulatory approval. In many countries, the carriers themselves were publicly owned. The basic argument against such structures of airline regulation and public ownership is, by now, a familiar one. Load factors tended to be low, profitability and service quality poor and fares high. Competition was all but eliminated by what can be regarded as regulatory failure, the traditional methods failing to secure efficient economic performances (Kay and Thompson, 1991; Sealy, 1992).

The global trend towards regulatory reform during the past two decades has accompanied the injection of more competitive conditions into economic activity generally. In many transport markets, suppliers have been progressively freed from price and entry constraints, while privatisation of state-owned assets has become commonplace. The regulatory changes affecting air transport have also been experienced in the bus, trucking and, if to a lesser extent, railway industries. Two general policy models can be identified. Deregulation refers to the exposure of transport modes to competitive laissez-faire, or free-market, forces, achieved through the removal of most regulatory controls over pricing, while permitting carriers to enter and leave markets at will. A second model, referred to variously as liberalisation or interventionism, recognises that the structure of transport industries may necessitate the retention of some form of regulatory protection, if consumers are to gain long-term benefits from the competition promoted by deregulatory measures. Whichever model is adopted, the two dimensions of the switch to free-market economics—regulatory freedom and privatisation— are held to work in tandem with each other. Proponents believe that privatisation without changes in economic regulation merely results in private monopolies, while liberalisation without privatisation only promotes state capitalism and the maintenance of inefficient public monopolies (Bannister and Button, 1991).

AIRLINE COMPETITION

Five facets of competition can be recognised within the airline industry (B. Graham, 1993a). Firstly, the popular conception of the term sees two or more carriers engaged in head-to-head confrontation while serving the same two airports. It is important to remember, however, that, as a result of bilateral agreements, many dually designated international routes actually function as interdependent duopolies, even if revenue is no longer pooled. The carriers still avoid competition by strategies such as complementary scheduling and frequencies, and identical tariff structures, particularly for full-cost tickets.

Secondly, two or more carriers may serve the same city-pairing but use different airports at one or both ends of the route. These circumstances can create a competitive niche market for a market entrant, a tactic used successfully by a number of carriers, notably Texas-based Southwest, currently the most profitable exponent of the deregulated US market. Although the airline has now expanded beyond its original markets, it initially established itself at Houston Hobby and Dallas Love Field, rather than Houston Intercontinental or Dallas/Fort Worth International. In much the same way, it is now developing operations out of Chicago Midway as an alternative to the much more heavily used O'Hare. However, if this strategy is to work successfully, airports must be capable of competing on equal terms which is often not the case.

Thirdly, deregulatory policies can increase the number of potential connections available to a consumer, particularly as airline networks have become reoriented around hub-and-spoke principles, which channel travellers through central hub airports where they change aircraft (see Chapter 6). This allows airlines to offer wide ranges of connections between secondary or non-hub cities, routes that might lack sufficient demand to support direct air services. If a city is a spoke on several competing networks of this type, the range of possible connections available to a traveller may be increased by the proliferation of hubs and the feeder networks serving them. In Europe, for example, carriers, such as BA, KLM, Lufthansa, Sabena and Air France, have created extensive domestic and short-haul feeder services from secondary cities which allow on-line connections through their hubs at London Heathrow, Amsterdam, Frankfurt, Brussels and Paris Charles de Gaulle (CDG). In the United States, the development of very large hub-and-spoke networks permits a multiplicity of similar city-pair connections.

Fourthly, if somewhat more obtusely, the introduction of deregulatory policies can lead to an increase in the number of carriers, thereby permitting the development of additional services out of previously under-utilised airports, which also provide niche markets for these airlines. While these may actually be monopoly services, consumers are still being offered alternative choices in public transport.

Finally, air transport is subject to inter-modal competition from private cars, long-distance coaches and, particularly, HSTs. The extent of such competition is highly variable at the global scale, depending upon the geography of the country and government policies for transport infrastructural investment. The best examples of rail competition are provided by Europe (see Chapter 14) and Japan, where newly built high-speed lines provide real alternatives to air transport on some city-pairings (Murayama, 1994). Conversely, in large countries, including Australia, the United States, Brazil or Russia, or those with a fractured geography such as Indonesia, the Philippines or Canada, air transport has a significant edge over terrestrial modes because of the time-savings that it can offer.

AIRLINE DEREGULATION AND LIBERALISATION

The first intimations of airline deregulation or liberalisation occurred during the 1970s as government agencies began to relax restrictions on fares and route authorities. In the United States, these early initiatives were codified into the 1978 legislation, which, in line with the legislation for other transport modes, removed federal control over airline market entry and exit and allowed prices and services to be determined by forces of market supply and demand (Button, 1989b; Pickrell, 1991). Subsequent results have been mixed. At best, the heavily contested evidence suggests that airline fares are now lower than they might otherwise have been, particularly for leisure passengers. For example, one calculation concludes that discount prices were reduced by 35 per cent between 1976–81, the welfare gain to consumers reaching $325m in 1981 alone. In contrast, deregulation has had no significant effect on business fares (Dresner and Tretheway, 1992). Moreover, business travellers have benefited from increased flight frequency and service convenience, partly attributable to the development of hub-and-spoke networks (Morrison and Winston, 1986; 1990). It is worth noting, however, that the CAB's regulatory structures, in force prior to 1978, were particularly restrictive compared to those in the United Kingdom and elsewhere. Consequently, the benefits of deregulation are bound to appear greater, one important factor militating against the uncritical acceptance of the US experience as a model for other countries.

Ultimately, however, consumer benefits have been eclipsed among the more visible repercussions of deregulation by the enormous financial losses incurred by the largest airlines, particularly during the early 1990s. These can be attributed to self-inflicted price wars and over-capacity, combined with recession and the effects of the Gulf War. Furthermore, there has been a marked attenuation of competition (Kahn, 1988). Following a period of intense rivalry, and the establishment of a number of new carriers, particularly during the early 1980s, a combination of merger, acquisition, predation and business failure has produced a dramatic increase in the size and route

networks of some incumbents, notably the mega-cart
United and Delta. Some commentators argue that this (
marked that, *de facto*, re-regulation has occurred, with the
the new regulators. In a swingeing attack on US-sty
Dempsey and Goetz (1992) conclude that the process wa
economic assumptions and that transportation is not a pt
industry. Thus, they claim that the US airline industry has become an
oligopoly. The eight largest US airlines now account for 95 per cent of the
domestic passenger market. Virtually all major hub airports are dominated
by a single airline, and almost two-thirds of airline city-pair markets are
monopolies (see Chapters 6 and 7).

Liberalisation, the alternative model of introducing competition to the
airline industry, is predicated upon the failure of deregulators to recognise
that their removal of control is in itself insufficient to overcome the inclina-
tion of incumbent suppliers to devise mechanisms which might blunt the
effects of actual or potential competition (Button, 1991). Thus, the rectifica-
tion of various kinds of market failure constitutes the primary rationale for
retaining interventionist mechanisms under a regime of liberalisation (Kay
and Vickers, 1990). In the airline industry, market failure can be equated
with monopoly, or the propensity to monopoly, for considered 'route-by-
route, the airline industry is incurably oligopolistic' (Pryke, 1987, p.79).
Thus, it can be argued that the prime objective of aviation policy is to
regulate the industry in order to promote competition and avoid the interdependence of such duopolies or oligopolies (Wheatcroft, 1988). Liberalisation
policies assume the necessity of continued intervention to protect and per-
petuate such competition.

As Kahn (1990) argues, the abolition of direct economic regulation is by no
means synonymous with the implementation of a *laissez-faire* regime. Deregulation itself can produce vested interests such as the mega-carriers.
Therefore, continued vigorous government intervention in the shape of anti-
trust legislation and controls on predation may be necessary. Thus, there
may well be a 'paradoxical emergence of extensive re-regulation of economic activity in a period supposedly typified by drastic deregulation' (G.
Thompson, 1990, p.135), although the form of such intervention may be
fundamentally different in character and intent to that which went before.

Dempsey and Goetz (1992) accuse Kahn of hypocrisy, arguing that the
removal of economic regulation inevitably subjects the air transport industry, and the public it serves, to all the disadvantages of a *laissez-faire* market.
In particular, they cite the attenuation of air services to smaller communities
and the inconvenience, increased journey times and greater costs to travellers incurred by routeings across hub airports. They argue that US-style
deregulation needs to be rolled back because government has to correct
market failure and protect those economic and social interests that do not
find a high priority in a free-market regime. For such reasons, virtually all

ernments, concerned to introduce competition into their national airline industries, have declined the US model and opted, instead, for some version of liberalisation. Policies following this paradigm have been applied, particularly to domestic services, in countries as diverse as Canada, Mexico, Australia, the Republic of South Africa, the United Kingdom, Japan, Taiwan and Korea, and also, as of 1993, within the EU. However, the results have again been unconvincing.

Canada's experiment in planned gradual liberalisation from 1988 onwards, a strategy that followed the UK rather than US example, has produced an Air Canada–Canadian Airlines International (Canadian) duopoly, both having since sought alliances with US carriers (Continental and American respectively) in order to help guarantee their future survival (Oum *et al.*, 1991). Almost all the small regional carriers in Canada are either affiliates or subsidiaries of these two companies. The problem lies in the country's geography. There are very few large markets outside the Toronto–Ottawa–Montreal corridor, a mere 25 city-pairs accounting for half the domestic market (Button, 1989a; Small, 1993). Canada may well provide an apposite illustration of the argument that the air transport market in many countries is too small to produce a competitive domestic industry (Putsay, 1992). Unlike the United States, very few countries have a sufficiently large internal air transport market to produce substantial on-line feed traffic that might improve the international competitiveness of its carriers. Nevertheless, several countries, including New Zealand and Chile, have applied deregulatory policies to limited or relatively small domestic markets. In both cases, the outcome has been the creation of duopolies (respectively Air New Zealand/Ansett New Zealand and Ladeco/LAN-Chile). In Mexico, the climate of economic liberalisation has encouraged a number of airlines to compete with the privatised but merged national carrier, AeroMexico/Mexicana.

In Europe, until many of its functions were superseded by changes in EU legislation in 1993, the CAA maintained a long-term policy that used route-licensing procedures to establish UK domestic and international competition to BA. Its aim was to create long-term user benefits and promote a profitable UK multi-airline industry. Although compromised by BA's largely successful counter-strategy, aimed at retaining its near-monopoly over UK air transport, and the not-unconnected business failure of many of the 'second-force' carriers sponsored by the CAA's regulatory intervention, British Midland (40 per cent owned by Scandinavian Airline System—SAS), Air UK (45 per cent owned by KLM) and Virgin remain as three of the few successful recent examples of market entry into the European scheduled airline business.

In advance of the inauguration of the Single European Market (SEM) in 1993, air transport within the EU was subjected to a trio of progressively more liberalised sets of reforms (see Table 8.1). The Third Package, implemented from 1 January 1993, allows airlines to set their own fares, subject to safeguards on predatory and excessive pricing. Perhaps the legislation's most significant element concerns the endorsement of the principle of general cabotage within the EU, the right of a Community airline to carry traffic between two points within a Member State, other than the one in which it is registered. This comes into force in 1997, after which an EU carrier can theoretically fly any routes that it chooses within the Community, apart from some regional city-pairings protected from competition under various provisions of the Third Package (B. Graham, 1992).

Elsewhere, deregulation of an Australian market, then dominated by two incumbents, Australian and Ansett, began in 1990. At that stage, the third major Australian carrier, Qantas, was precluded from operating domestic services. One entrant, Compass Airlines, was prepared for entry on to the major trunk routes in advance of the legislatory changes; in the event, the carrier survived almost exactly one year. A reborn Compass also went bankrupt. Since then, the Australian government has reshaped the industry. A privatised Qantas acquired Australian, allowing it to operate domestic services in competition with Ansett, which in turn has been allowed to break Qantas's international monopoly. The net result of Australian deregulation is the replacement of one duopoly by another.

In addition to Australia and New Zealand, several other Asian-Pacific countries have implemented deregulatory policies for both domestic and international routes. Currently, this is, and will remain, the world's most dynamic air transport market, a factor encouraging the appearance of several well financed and equipped entrants. For example, the Taiwanese flag-carrier, China Airlines, now faces substantial competition from EVA Air, while Asiana has emerged as a potent competitor to Korean Air. The Japanese carriers, All Nippon and Japan Air System, have been permitted to extend their domestic competition with JAL on to international routes. Several small carriers have also entered the Indonesian, Indian and Pakistani domestic markets in competition with the state airlines.

In summary, therefore, outside the United States, wherever airlines actually compete on city-pairings, the application of liberalising policies has generally seen the replacement of monopolies by duopolies on some domestic and international services. As noted earlier, this is not inconsistent with competition, given the naturally oligopolistic nature of air transport. The 'key point is not how many airline companies serve the market, but rather the degree and nature of competition which exists between them' (Button, 1989b, p.197). However, the extent of increased competition is limited, particularly for international services. Despite more liberal ASAs, governments, even those ostensibly committed to the introduction of market forces, remain firmly committed to national interests. In much of the world, third- and fourth-freedom capacities and frequencies remain regulated, and single designation of carriers still prevails. Fifth-freedom rights can still be relatively rare. A protectionism born of national political and economic considerations, continues to be a dominant characteristic of international air transport.

PRIVATISATION

The changing regulatory framework for air transport is part of the global dominion of the economic principles of the neo-liberal New Right which emphasise the use of market forces to achieve policy objectives. In the United Kingdom, for example, this was expressed in a clash between the neo-liberal imperative of 'rolling-back' the state, and a Conservative ideology, more concerned with the maintenance of social and moral values. Arguably, the ensuing neo-liberal ascendancy ensured that the successful attainment of the financial and ideological rewards of privatisaticn emerged as the flagship project of the Thatcherite government, outweighing the suppression of competition involved (Kay and Thompson, 1986; Swann, 1988). Although the promotion of competition and the privatisation of state-owned assets in the airline and other industries are linked ideologically, the policies devised to achieve these goals may be mutually conflicting.

Critics have argued that the neo-liberal wing of the New Right will compromise competition to defeat all things collectivist (G. Thompson, 1990). The privatisation of BA was first announced in 1979, but the carrier's finances were in such a poor condition that the process was long postponed: the lengthy law suits which ensued from Laker's 1982 collapse, brought about in part by allegedly predatory activity on the part of its international rivals—including BA—further delayed the process. In the interim, BA's finances were reconstructed and it was finally sold off in 1986–7. However, the airline remains a largely ambiguous presence in the UK air transport industry. The UK government's insistence that the market value of BA remained unimpaired prior to the airline's privatisation in 1987 proved to be one of the most significant factors undermining the CAA's policy of promoting more competition within the UK airline industry. The involvement of the UK government in negotiating more liberal bilaterals during the 1980s may have had something to do with its commitment to competition, but it was also arguably in the national interest if that is defined by the privatisation of BA (Pelkmans, 1986). The ambiguity continues: although now a private company, BA remains the UK's *de facto* flag-carrier and the principal beneficiary of the government's bilateral negotiations with other countries. It uses its powerful public-relations operation to remain close to government and has contributed to Conservative Party funds. All this is best symbolised, perhaps, by the Concorde aircraft, paid for by UK taxpayers but used by this private company as one of its most powerful advertising tools (B. Graham, 1994).

While the ideological push to privatise airlines and airports was far stronger in the United Kingdom than elsewhere (Bell and Cloke. 1990), there has still been a notable world-wide retreat from state ownership of airlines. Some 30–40 airlines had moved away from state ownership by 1990, and more have since followed (Wheatcroft and Lipman, 1990). As in the United

Kingdom, privatisation can take a radical form in which state-owned assets, especially nationalised airlines, route rights and slots at capacity-restricted airports, are transferred to private firms. However, privatisation is much more likely to be a less ideologically-inspired policy, involving the sale of part of a state airline's capital to the private sector. Although the state may well be a minority shareholder after privatisation, its shares give it greater powers than those accruing to ordinary equity holders (Rapp and Vellas, 1992).

Privatisation is thus more likely to be an empirical, pragmatic process, concerned with achieving greater efficiency and competitiveness among carriers. It can provide a means of catering for the financial needs of an airline, while allowing governments to avoid the huge costs of retaining non-market-oriented philosophies in contemporary international airline operations (Putsay, 1992). A dramatic example of the costs involved occurred in 1993–4, when the French, Greek, Irish and Portuguese governments were forced to spend around $7.3 billion on EC-approved subsidies to their ailing flag-carriers, an amount almost twice as large as the entire losses made by the airline industry globally during 1993. Clearly, such payments distort the competitive process if privately owned airlines, which must make profits on their investments or exit the market, have to compete with subsidised state-controlled airlines. In 1993, the EC established the *Comité des Sages* to examine competitiveness in the European airline industry. Its subsequent report recommended the adoption of a 'one time–last time' approach to state aid, with strict conditions attached to these payments in order to safeguard the interests of competitors. It remains to be seen, however, if the EC will enforce these recommendations (see Chapter 8).

Full or partial privatisation has been a common feature of many world airlines during the past decade. BA and JAL, the two largest state-owned carriers (apart from Aeroflot), were both fully privatised in 1987, as were Mexicana and Air Canada in 1988 and 1989 respectively. Elsewhere, privatisation measures are being applied to carriers as diverse as SAS, Royal Jordanian, Sudan Airways, Malaysia Airlines and Singapore Airlines. Various governments have also sold substantial shareholdings in publicly owned carriers to other airlines. Iberia, for example, albeit state-owned and virtually bankrupt, holds 84 per cent of Aerolineas Argentinas and 40 per cent of Viasa, while BA acquired 25 per cent of Qantas when the Australian carrier was partially privatised in 1992. When Air New Zealand was privatised no less than three foreign carriers—Qantas, American and JAL—took shares, thus simultaneously creating three key strategic alliances (Putsay, 1992).

A very particular form of privatisation has occurred throughout Eastern Europe and the former Soviet Union. Under Marxist–Leninist governments, these economies were not market-oriented, while airlines were supplied exclusively with Soviet-built equipment (D. Hall, 1993a and b; Symons,

1993). Outside the USSR, there was little domestic air transport, most routes being international services within the Soviet bloc. Since 1989, the Eastern European carriers have entered upon a traumatic period of restructuring. Aeroflot has been divided into a whole series of smaller state and privately owned companies. Malev (Hungary), CSA (Czechoslovak Airlines, renamed Czech Airlines in March 1995), LOT-Polish Airlines (LOT) and Balkan Bulgarian are being partially privatised, a process which has involved equity sales to foreign carriers (see Chapter 8).

Conversely, some governments have been loath to promote privatisation. While this is often attributed to base motives, particularly nationalistically inspired protectionism, there is a case for retaining state control of transport infrastructure. Although the involvement of the private sector in the financing of transport investments and the operation of transport services may be a desirable aim in the promotion of more efficient and competitive operations (Bannister and Button, 1991), transport also involves notions of social equity and democratic access to services. Air transport infrastructure can be viewed, not as a free-standing sector of the economy but as one component in an array of factors involved in social and economic development. Thus, public service imperatives may override free-market economics, one of the claimed reasons for the French government's obstinacy in permitting domestic competition to *Groupe* Air France.

REGULATORY AGENCIES AND AIR TRANSPORT

AIRLINE INDUSTRY REGULATORS

As observed above, the introduction of a more competitive environment for air transport has not removed the need for regulation. In Europe generally, and particularly in the United Kingdom, privatisation of monopolies or quasi-monopolies such as BA has been followed by reregulation, a 'renaissance of intervention' (G. Thompson, 1990, p.135). Every country retains a regulatory agency with responsibility for air transport. The monitoring of safety standards alone will demand the continuation of some form of regulatory intervention, one reason why air carriers still have to seek operating licences. Furthermore, continued regulation may also be necessary because the dramatic disparities of size and influence, so characteristic of the world airline industry, provide ample scope for predatory behaviour.

The CAA is one example of an airline industry regulator (B. Graham, 1994). It is a specialised agency, possessing its own formidable research and data-collection facility, and thus capable of fact-finding, rule-making and enforcement. A command over statistical data relating to the UK's air transport industry is an essential prerequisite to its regulatory role, providing a detailed empirical basis for its judgements on, and administration of, competing private companies. Essentially, a regulator such as the CAA can be viewed as a mediator among the often conflicting demands of the four interest groups involved in air transport: government, consumers, the airline industry and itself. Kay and Vickers (1990) provide a model of the two basic means by which such a regulator can influence the behaviour of an industry (Figure 3.2). It can regulate the structure of the industry by using route-licensing to place restrictions on entry and/or regulate the behaviour of the industry through price controls and measures against anti-competitive conduct. Prior to the implementation of the EC's Third Package in 1993, the CAA did both, as was also true of the CAB in the United States prior to 1978. With the advent of EU liberalisation, the CAA has relinquished many of its controls over UK airlines, although it remains responsible for route-licensing of extra-community air services and monitoring the financial fitness of airline operators. Although the function has now passed to the EC, the CAA also had a responsibility to protect airlines from predation.

In company with most regulators, however, the CAA found it 'hard enough to reach an acceptable definition of predatory behaviour, let alone detect and deter it' (Kay and Vickers, 1990, p.235), although it has been active in attempting to protect consumers from excessive fares, one form of anti-competitive behaviour (Hanlon, 1994). The CAA defines predation by one airline against another as activities 'actuated by malice'. In the event, few cases have been brought before it for consideration, perhaps because of the difficulty of finding evidence to meet the terms of the definition. Robert Ayling, now chief financial officer of BA, provides a more cynical, if realistic, definition of anti-competitive behaviour: 'a good rule-of-thumb test is whether the company would be embarrassed by public disclosure of any action which might adversely affect a competitor' (cited in Gregory, 1994, pp.224–5).

Precisely because BA has been publicly embarrassed on several occasions, the UK airline industry offers several examples of the ways in which anti-competitive behaviour can occur. First, in 1982, Laker Airways collapsed after a cartel of international airlines, including BA, Pan Am, TWA, Lufthansa, Swissair and SAS, simultaneously slashed their North Atlantic fares in a successful bid to undercut Laker's low-cost 'Skytrain' concept. Although BA has always denied any guilt, the Laker liquidator's case was settled out-of-court in 1985; around half the settlement fund was paid by BA, and the demands of all creditors were met. A US criminal investigation was dropped at the direct request of President Reagan, following a personal intervention by Margaret Thatcher; BA could not be privatised while the case was outstanding.

Secondly, in 1993, in addition to paying libel damages of £0.6 million, BA was forced to apologise publicly in the London High Court to its small rival, Virgin. BA had been involved in a series of unethical business practices, including the illegal accessing of computer records, which aimed at destroying Virgin's reputation, customer base and financial credibility. It has since

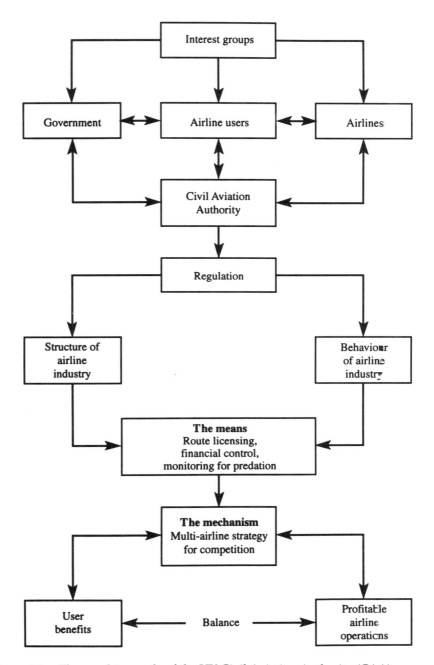

Figure 3.2. The regulatory role of the UK Civil Aviation Authority (CAA)
Source: B. Graham, 1994

been suggested that BA used similar methods to help undermine Air Europe, which collapsed in 1991 (Gregory, 1994). However, in neither example was the CAA, as the industry regulator, able to exert any significant control over apparently predatory activities. Indeed, no complaints in respect of either case were ever brought before it. This suggests that it is easier for such an agency to regulate the structure of an airline industry than control its behaviour.

THE REGULATION OF MERGER AND ACQUISITION

The difficulties, both legal and evidential, encountered by airline industry regulators in defining and recognising predation, clearly constitute a competitive advantage for established airlines, particularly large ones. This is compounded by the ambivalence displayed by other regulatory agencies towards merger and acquisition. The air transport industry in any country is subject to that state's legislation on monopolies and mergers and to the authority of the regulatory agencies charged with enforcing it. Increasingly, however, the global airline business is being reshaped by merger and acquisition, a trend particularly characteristic of the post-deregulation US industry (Dempsey and Goetz, 1992).

Several negative consequences can be identified. Some US take-overs were engineered through leveraged buy-outs in which speculators bought control of airlines, using funds largely provided by the companies themselves. The carriers involved have been saddled with enormous debts, very unhealthy debt/equity ratios and credit ratings to match. Eastern, the fourth largest US airline in 1978, collapsed entirely in 1991, following its leveraged buy-out by Texas Air in 1986. Other repercussions of merger and acquisition include the concentration of the US domestic market into the hands of the mega-carriers and the emergence of the 'fortress' hub airport. The US Department of Transportation (USDoT) has approved every airline merger submitted to it since it took over the CAB's regulatory role in this respect at the beginning of 1985 (Dempsey and Goetz, 1992).

However, this blanket approval of merger has not been extended to foreign interests wishing to invest in US airlines. The USDoT continues to legislate to prevent them acquiring more than 49 per cent of the shares in US airlines (increased from 25 per cent in 1991) and no more than 25 per cent of voting stock. Nor can they otherwise control the company. The President's National Commission (1993) did suggest that privatised airlines from countries signing liberal bilaterals be allowed up to 49 per cent voting equity in US carriers. Examples of foreign carriers investing in US airlines include Air Canada's stake in Continental, BA's 25 per cent holding in USAir and KLM's stockholding in Northwest.

In Europe, too, neither the national regulatory authorities nor the EC have displayed any enthusiasm for preventing airline mergers and acquisitions.

Transnational acquisition is also much more liberalised than in the United States. Thus, the larger European carriers, notably BA and Lufthansa, have been acquiring equity in smaller airlines, both in their own countries and elsewhere. The EC approved the 1990 Air France take-over of UTA which also gave the flag-carrier control of Air Inter, the country's major domestic operator. The only condition was that Air France had to relinquish its 35 per cent stake in TAT European Airlines (TAT), the next most important French domestic airline. Ironically, it has since been acquired by BA, which is using the airline as a means of entering the French market. Furthermore, the EC also approved Air France's – and subsequently Swissair's – purchases of equity in Sabena.

Finally, mergers and acquisitions are not the only means of creating strategic alliances (see Chapter 5). A 1995 survey, which did not claim to be comprehensive, identified no fewer than 330 different alliances, involving 153 airlines (*Airline Business*, June 1995). Almost one-third of these involved equity holdings, the remainder relating to arrangements such as joint flights, code-sharing, shared ground-handling and catering activities and joint FFPs. A majority of all alliances had been entered into after January 1992. Code-sharing offers significant advantages to airlines. It permits them to use parts of each other's networks, thereby increasing the range of destinations and services offered by an individual airline. Further, it helps rationalise capacity, restricts competition and provides one means of circumventing bilateral constraints. Indeed, alliances of this sort represent one important means by which small carriers can protect their market. Until recently, regulatory authorities have taken little interest in arrangements of this type, apart from ensuring, as in the BA/USAir alliance, that they do not contravene national regulations on equity ownership or the conditions of bilateral agreements. However, code-sharing in particular is becoming politically more sensitive and in late 1994, for example, the EC announced that it was to investigate the anti-competitive implications of airline marketing alliances.

AIR TRANSPORT AND ITS ROLE IN BROADER ECONOMIC AND SOCIAL POLICIES

These issues need be mentioned only briefly here because they are more fully developed in Chapter 5. The extent of political interventionism into the operation and regulation of air transport partially reflects contrasting governmental priorities concerning the role played by the transport sector within wider policies addressing the geographically uneven patterning of social and economic development. Traditionally, it was argued that the regulation of transport markets was in the 'public interest', although this is a somewhat ambiguous concept. While it can be defined as the containment of monopoly power, comprehensive transport provision is also important for social equity reasons and in helping to integrate geographically diverse countries. When the transport industry is characterised by inter-modal competition, public interest can be defined as the controls necessary to ensure stability in the market place. Finally, economic regulation can be a means of protecting people from the externalities—including the danger of accidents, noise and environmental pollution—produced by the transport sector.

Common to all these public-interest approaches is the assumption that defects in market operations are likely to be greater than the problems of designing and operating suitable regulatory systems (Bannister and Button, 1991). Such ideas are associated ideologically with demand-oriented Keynesian economics and their emphasis upon the interventionist role of the state in the interests of society as a whole. Central to this reasoning is the argument that states evolve systems of regional transfer of resources and wealth for other than economic reasons. However, the emergence of the New Right during the 1970s meant that Keynesian ideas of social welfare, largely anathema in the United States since the New Deal, were questioned in Europe too, particularly in the United Kingdom. The Thatcherite accession to power in 1979 began an era of market-dominated economic policy in which concerns of social equity became subservient to the pursuit of profit, albeit addressed in terms of personal freedom.

Many European and Asian governments have been more reticent about adopting relatively unconstrained market economics. Much of the debate concerning the extent of state intervention into the transport sector in general and the airline industry in particular relates to the differing priorities which individual governments ascribe to the maket. On one hand, it can be argued that, under regulation, air transport users were paying high fares, either for poor service or for service qualities which they did not necessarily desire (Keeler, 1991). Thus, many governments in Europe and elsewhere have attempted to legislate for more competitive airline industries that can at least offer consumers a better range and flexibility in fares and services.

Conversely, air transport cannot be ring-fenced and at least three impediments to a fully market-based solution can be identified. First, airline networks will contain a substantial number of routes on which continued service, although unprofitable, may be desirable for social equity reasons and also because the routes contribute to improved aircraft utilisation and hub feed (see Chapter 4). In periods of industry retrenchment, such loss-making routes could be abandoned, although that might conflict with the wider aims of social equity policy. Alternatively, the services can be supported by cross-subsidies from more profitable routes or even by direct subsidy from regional or central governments.

Secondly, air transport is a major employer, not only in the airlines themselves but also in ground services, airports and aerospace manufacturers. It is all too easy to forget that the converse of a euphemism such as 'over peopling' (in the sense of over-employment) is redundancy and unemployment. Between 1992–4, for example, European airlines cut 30 000 jobs, leading transport unions to argue that the EC has gone too far in liberalising civil aviation. They contend that the airlines' problems are self-inflicted, stemming from 'ruinous competition . . . and . . . creation of overcapacity'. Thus, they believe that the EC should analyse the social and economic consequences of deregulation for those working in the industry, rather than restricting its remit to seeking ways of making the airlines more competitive (*Aviation Europe*, 10 March 1994).

Thirdly, the EC, EU constituent states and many individual governments elsewhere remain committed to political policies, designed to offset the dis-benefits of uneven development and peripherality. It is apparent that the free market cannot overcome the economic and social divergence of regions and the resultant inequality in the distribution of opportunity. Further, states evolve systems of regional transfer for other than economic reasons; governments attempt to create stability and identity through engendering a sense of belonging in the peripheries. Economic benefits, channelled through regional policies, are the cement of social stability and national integration (MacKay, 1993). Within the EU, for example, the creation of the single market has reinforced the advantages of central location. There is imperfect mobility of capital and labour, and processes of convergence have been counterbalanced by the peripheral additions of Ireland, Portugal and Greece (A. Williams, 1994). Nevertheless, convergence remains a stated aim of the Single European Act. However, the peripheral regions, the poorest within the EU in per capita terms, also experience the greatest costs for business air travel to the core. Therefore, a tension exists between the concept of convergence (essentially Keynesian), and the competitiveness objectives of the EC (essentially New Right), as exemplified for air transport in the report of the *Comité des Sages*. In effecting any resolution to this conflict of priorities, it can be argued that, due to its quasi-public utility nature, the transportation industry requires continuing enlightened regulation to protect the wider public interest (Dempsey and Goetz, 1992).

CONCLUSIONS

Therefore, the linkages between politics and the air transport industry are characterised by conflicts of interest and by competing priorities. National self-interest is often at odds with the introduction of a more competitive environment for air transport; the airline industry is inherently prone to oligopoly, while measures promoting increased competition may be compromised by an undue emphasis on privatisation. Full-blown ideologically driven privatisation on the UK model is neither necessary nor even desirable in the promotion of competition. Pragmatic partial privatisation allows governments to effect continued intervention into airline operations in pursuit of wider national interests, while maintaining the consumer benefits that accrue from increased competition. The direction of causation may be from increased efficiency to privatisation rather than the converse. It appears that continuing regulation, particularly of merger, acquisition and predatory behaviour, is required if there is to be effective competition at the national level, while the promotion of a more competitive industry may conflict with policies aimed at enhancing social and economic equity within a state.

4   The Economics of Air Transport

At best, the air transport industry is one characterised by only the most modest economic returns on capital invested. In 1992, for example, the world's top 50 carriers, responsible for about 80 per cent of the industry's total turnover, lost an estimated $5 billion on their international scheduled services alone and $7.5 billion when all activities within airline groups were taken into account. Although the 1993 statistics were better, global losses still amounted to $4.1 billion. Only one-third of the top 30 carriers recorded a profit. The modest $1 billion profits predicted by IATA for 1994 contrast with cumulative losses of at least $15 billion incurred since 1990. Although the magnitude of these figures is partially attributable to factors external to the air transport industry, they can also be explained by the nature and behaviour of the airlines themselves as they attempt to come to terms with a competitive and privatised environment.

This chapter examines the most important economic characteristics of the airline industry which, in conjunction with the political factors discussed in Chapter 3, are fundamental to an understanding of the geography of air service provision world-wide. Furthermore, they help account for the limited success of political policies aimed at attaining a more competitive airline industry.

Four sets of economic characteristics are examined:

(i)   the compromise between capacity, yields, costs and market share;
(ii) air transport as a contestable industry—sunk costs, the difficulties of market entry and the significance of frequency;
(iii) the strategic advantages of incumbency;
(iv) additional barriers to market entry.

CAPACITY, YIELDS, COSTS AND MARKET SHARE

During the 1980s, airlines world-wide ordered or acquired options on large numbers of new aircraft. Because of long lead-in times in manufacturing, such orders have to be based on projected rather than actual demand. By 1990, the airlines' total commitment extended to around 2500 aircraft, worth some $150 billion. Many of these aircraft were purchased by specialist leasing companies, the two largest being GPA/GE Capital Aviation Services (formerly the GPA Group), based at Shannon, Ireland, and the International

Lease Finance Corporation of Los Angeles. In order to fill this capacity, and finance the purchase or leasing of equipment, the airline industry required continued world economic growth during the 1990s. Instead, advanced economies went into recession, most deeply in Europe but also in North America and even Asia-Pacific, where Japan in particular has been badly effected. The economic downturn was compounded by the market-depressing effects of the Gulf War.

Consequently, airlines have faced a mismatch between capacity and demand, a difficulty further exacerbated by the aggregate results of their individual reactions to this problem. One obvious response was for airlines to accept the financial penalties involved and defer or cancel unnecessary capacity. Many of the aircraft ordered in the 1980s will never be delivered. Again, airlines have speeded up the retirement of older equipment; in 1994, almost 1000 airliners were in storage, many parked in the western US deserts. Most of these planes are unlikely to fly again. Airlines also moved to cut costs, particularly wages, which account for 25–35 per cent of the total operating costs of international carriers (Doganis, 1991). However, these measures were insufficient to stem the increasing losses.

Therefore, carriers, desperate to fill spare capacity during the early 1990s, resorted to marginal pricing policies—or fare wars. The classic industry problem is the instantly perishable nature of its product. As soon as an aircraft is pushed back from its departure gate, the unsold goods—empty seats—have no value at all. However, the marginal costs of filling at least some of those seats—cabin service and a minimal amount of fuel—are so low, that it may be better for an individual carrier to sell them at virtually any price, even though this will not cover the long-term and fixed costs involved (Dempsey and Goetz, 1992). Therefore, despite weak underlying demand through much of the early 1990s, particularly for business travel, airlines diluted yield—the operating revenue gained per revenue tonne-kilometre flown—by heavily discounting fares. The chase for market share became the principal aggregate response to over-capacity.

Several other factors inhibiting the retrenchment of services have further contributed to the creation of over-capacity. Generous bankruptcy laws, particularly the US Chapter 11 provisions, and continued state subsidies, most notably from certain European governments, have worked against reductions in capacity because bankrupt carriers have remained in the market-place. Again, runway slots are in scarce supply at many airports and airlines must continue to occupy them, making it difficult to reduce the frequency of services, although smaller aircraft can be substituted to reduce capacity. Finally, continued regulatory restrictions, particularly on international services, make it very difficult for a carrier to move capacity from weak to strong markets (EC, 1994b).

The issue of yield has to be treated carefully, however, because it is affected by sector distance (short- or long-haul), the airline's involvement in freight and its marketing strategy. Therefore, low yields are not necessarily a weakness, the highly profitable Singapore Airlines being one notable example of a low-yield carrier. The critical factor then becomes very high load factors which equate to good yield management. The key to economic survival seems to be low unit costs rather than yields *per se*. In general terms, high-yield carriers tend to have high costs and low-yield airlines low costs (Doganis *et al.*, 1994). The evidence suggests that costs do decrease eventually following deregulation, principally due to increased total factor productivity (Formby *et al.*, 1990). Non-US airlines, for example, may have lower labour costs but US companies have better levels of productivity, the result of higher traffic density (Windle, 1991).

Consequently, the economics of an airline depend on the complex relationships between market share, costs and yield. The latter reflects the nature of the traffic mix carried. As discussed in Chapter 2, scheduled passenger air transport is a segmented market, divided crudely between high-yield business and low-yield leisure travellers. Thus, from an airline's perspective, other things being equal, certain market segments are preferable to others because they produce higher yield. For example, 70 per cent of BA's income derives from its business market, which accounts for only 30 per cent of the airline's traffic. Nevertheless, profitably accessing this premium segment still requires low unit costs, particularly since it carries certain yield-diluting risks for the carriers, largely because the behaviour of the business market can depress load factors.

As observed in Chapter 2, business travellers demand ticketing and scheduling flexibility, leading to significant levels of cancellations and 'no-shows'. Airlines stand to lose the income of such seats completely because they are not prepared to subject business-class passengers to the financial penalties applied to those cancelling low-yield leisure tickets. In their yield-management programmes, airlines have developed three strategies to deal with this problem and its negative effects upon load factor. Firstly, they consciously overbook aircraft. Secondly, late-availability restricted tickets are offered to those leisure travellers prepared to risk inconvenience for low price. Thirdly, blocks of seats are passed on to 'bucket shops', now more grandly known as consolidators, for discount sale. Despite these tactics, the average passenger load factor for IATA carriers in 1993 was only 66 per cent (see Table 14.3). Consequently, empty seats are an inevitable repercussion of the interaction between the business segment and airline marketing practices, a factor of considerable relevance to the debate on infrastructure provision for air transport and the industry's environmental impact.

Normally, however, it is likely that most price-elastic low-yield capacity will be sold earlier. An airline, refraining from chasing market share at the expense of yield, could probably sell more seats of this type but will restrict their availability. However, during the early 1990s, most carriers responded to recession and the Gulf War by going for market volume. Relatively high traffic growth occurred in the North American, North Atlantic and European markets but, because yields fell, this was unprofitable for the airlines. Belatedly, by 1993–4, as the developed world moved out of recession and the market improved, more carriers were opting for higher-yield, premium traffic, combined with more efficient yield management and lower costs, rather than gross market share alone. Products were being up-graded, low-yield capacity was being marketed more effectively (for example, BA's 'World Offers' scheme), fleets were being downsized and more labour was being laid-off. Nevertheless, attempts to promote a more competitive world airline industry are compromised by even more basic factors, intrinsic to the very structure of the industry. In many ways, over-capacity, fare wars and low yields result from the inevitable attempts made by incumbents to subvert market entry by potential rivals, reflecting the increasingly competitive liberalised or deregulated environments in which the world's airlines are now operating.

THE CONTESTABLE MARKET, SUNK COSTS, MARKET ENTRY AND FREQUENCY

CONTESTABILITY AND SUNK COSTS

To a large extent, the academic justification of airline deregulation depends upon the theory of the contestable market, one in which an entrant has access to all the production techniques available to incumbents. Thus, entry decisions can be reversed without cost, and there are no barriers to wooing incumbent firms' customers (Baumol, 1982). It is important to remember that its proponents view this notion of contestability as a theoretical state rather than a description of reality (Button, 1989b) and that, further, it evolved subsequent to the 1978 deregulation of the US airline industry. It is argued that the scheduled airline industry is likely to be contestable because of two critical qualities. In the first instance, it is held to be characterised by low sunk costs, the non-recoverable costs incurred by a firm in entering a market. Secondly, this ensures that the threat of competition alone should be sufficient to modify the behaviour of incumbents (Alamdari and Black, 1992).

The proponents of contestability have generally recognised that sunk costs are a barrier to market entry but argue that the key factor is 'the smallness of the airlines' sunk costs relative to their fixed costs' (Baumol et al., 1982, p.282). A sunk cost is defined as any factor requiring expenditure by a new entrant into an industry while imposing no equivalent costs upon an incumbent. Subsequent empirical evidence, not least the failure of more than 150 entrant airlines between 1978–89, has encouraged the conclusion that the barriers and costs encountered in entering the US airline market are more substantial than theory originally suggested. Thus, it has been increasingly recognised that contestability theory is not a good predictor of the air transport market, the literature variously describing the industry as 'imperfectly contestable', 'workably competitive' or 'broadly oligopolistic'.

For its advocates, however, such provisos do not constitute an argument against deregulation. They argue that this remains worthwhile despite the absence of perfect contestability, citing the admittedly contested American evidence to argue that the performance of the industry is better than it was under regulation (Keeler, 1991). Thus Levine (1987), for example, concludes that although the airline industry is naturally a non-competitive oligopoly, entry barriers remain sufficiently low to make competition workable. Those he identifies include: the costs of providing information to travellers and monitoring the behaviour of travel agents; the investment required in creating a brand-name and reputation in the market-place; and, finally, schemes that induce brand loyalty.

The theory of contestability envisaged a situation in which an airline market was vulnerable to hit-and-run, or costlessly reversible, entry. Consequently, an incumbent could prevent entry only by offering the public the same benefits that competition would otherwise have introduced (Baumol *et al.*, 1982). Although an airline entering a market has substantial fixed capital costs, it was argued that, largely, these do not constitute sunk costs. The major element of capital—aircraft—can be recovered from a particular market with little or no cost, hence the expression, 'capital on wings'. For a large airline, simply adding a route to an existing network, these conditions may apply. The aircraft, personnel and marketing structure will already be in place and, consequently, route entry incurs only the minimal marginal costs arising from actually placing passengers in seats.

In assessing the validity of these arguments, it is important to distinguish among the differing conditions of market entry because these have significant repercussions for the relative impact of entry barriers upon airlines. An early analysis (Caves, 1962) concluded that there were substantial impediments to the creation of a competing trunk network but only moderate barriers to entry on to a single route. However, this is likely to apply only if the carrier is already serving the cities at either end of the route. In a survey of 281 new US market entries during part of 1980, Berry (1990) found that the entrant already served both end-points in 245 cases and at least one in 277 instances. Such additional services do not have to be profitable in themselves in order to benefit an airline financially. Any income will make a contribution to fixed costs already incurred, less the additional marginal costs of the new service. In the actuality of airline operations, carriers of all sizes enter markets for this reason, seeking routes that improve aircraft and personnel utilisation rather than necessarily possessing much actual profit potential in themselves.

Nevertheless, it is best not to be too sanguine about entry barriers, even for existing firms setting up new routes. The airline industry globally is characterised by enormous imbalances of carrier size which may mean that a putative entrant to a market can be moving into conflict with a very much larger competitor, a factor that magnifies the importance of entry barriers and increases their costs. An entirely new airline may face even more rigorous barriers to entry. However, Gelman and Salop (1983) propose a model in which the entrant uses the size of the dominant firm to its own advantage. The entrant voluntarily restricts its market share so that it is too costly for the incumbent to match its lower fares. This strategy, in which the entrant may survive if it can offer the incumbent a large enough share of the total market, effectively describes that adopted by several of the 'start-up' carriers entering the US domestic market since 1992 (see Chapter 7).

Advocates of a competitive airline industry do envisage more dynamic processes of market entry, ones that would lead to competing carriers generating consumer benefits relating to fares, service and frequency on the same airport and city-pairings. As observed above, however, it has become obvious since the implementation of US deregulation that airline markets are at least imperfectly contested. Sunk costs may be sunk in ways not previously evident, nor do they have to be large to allow incumbents to enjoy significant advantages. They include the provision of terminal and maintenance facilities, sales promotion, route development and air crew training costs (Lazar, 1989). Such sunk costs may indeed be comparatively modest, being concerned primarily with assembling an airline operation and commissioning its start-up (Beesley, 1986). Even for a new carrier, the most important physical plant—the aircraft—is normally a relatively low-cost element in terms of capital because it can be leased. If the venture fails, the aircraft is returned to the lessor. Nevertheless, while monetary outlay may be comparatively modest, sunk costs can be regarded as symptoms of more complex problems, being only part of a family of absolute barriers to entry (McGowan and Seabright, 1989). As discussed in the subsequent section, incumbency confers an array of important market advantages to airlines. Three further reasons can be identified which explain why an emphasis on sunk costs alone radically underestimates the difficulties of market entry.

First, because the airline market has proved to be imperfectly contestable, evidence suggests that potential or threatened entry into a market is ineffective in achieving more competitive air services. Actual entry is essential in order to modify the behaviour of incumbents. In the United States, for example, it has been shown that airlines adjust their pricing strategies to the actual competitive conditions on each route (Oum *et al.*, 1993). In Europe, the only airport-pairings characterised by price, service and frequency competition are those few served by a third carrier such as British Midland on routes including London Heathrow to Paris, Brussels, Amsterdam and Frankfurt (CAA, 1993c). Otherwise, despite the implementation of the Third Package on airline liberalisation, the characteristic scheduled intra-European city-pairing remains serviced by two carriers, charging very similar fares and operating largely complementary schedules with similarly sized aircraft. The situation on intercontinental routes is even less competitive (CAA, 1994b).

Secondly, many—if not most—airlines have less than perfect information concerning the markets that they are attempting to enter. The profit potential of a route will be confidential to incumbents and, while load factors can be calculated from passenger uplift and frequency statistics, vital information such as yield per passenger will not be available. Traffic forecasting is far from being an exact decision at the best of times, even for the largest carriers. As the UK route-licensing procedures operated by the CAA prior to 1993 demonstrated, the traffic-forecasting techniques employed by small airlines may be particularly unsophisticated, estimates of passenger numbers being no more than calculations of the traffic volumes required from routes rather than representing any considered assessments of likely demand. Ultimately, the only testing ground for the traffic forecast is the market.

Finally, it is less than clear that sunk costs constitute the most important factor in the economics of airline entry on to a route. In the United Kingdom, the CAA has been concerned that airlines enter routes on the basis of long-term investment decisions, which are the antithesis of the theoretical concept of hit-and-run, or costlessly reversible, entry. In order to protect the long-term consumer and supplier benefits to be gained from a more competitive airline industry, the CAA has expected airlines to examine route economics on the basis of fully allocated costs, even if it has 'no uniquely correct way' of allocating such costs to individual routes. Fully allocated costs include everything connected with the provision of air service. For an existing carrier a new service will benefit the airline's overall finances because a proportion of fixed costs can be reallocated away from other routes. Obviously, these advantages do not accrue to a new carrier.

MARKET SEGMENTATION AND THE IMPORTANCE OF FREQUENCY

Leaving aside these difficulties, advocates of deregulation envisage lower-cost entrants gaining market share by undercutting the prices charged by incumbents. However, the segmented nature of the product sold by airlines must also be considered (see Chapter 3). Low-yield leisure traffic is price elastic, small changes in price having a substantial impact on demand. Conversely, a fall in price for business travel does not generate substantial new demand, a factor militating against a low-fare entry strategy by an airline seeking a high-yield market. It does mean, however, that a successful low-cost entrant could be more profitable than a higher-cost incumbent.

These particular characteristics of market segmentation are crucial in determining an airline's strategy for market entry and, moreover, help account for the singular lack of success, both in North America and Europe, of scheduled airlines that depend on cost leadership policies. With the notable exception of Southwest, the virtual disappearance of the first wave of low-cost, 'no-frills' airlines, which developed in the wake of US deregulation, suggests that carriers, opting to compete by lowering operating costs and fares, are highly vulnerable, particularly as older airlines have been able to adjust costs downwards. Southwest has established a large niche market, demonstrating that unit costs can be kept low if the frequency of flights in the system is maintained at a high level. Therefore, it has to generate substantial load factors in markets that create extensive demand, often using airports served by other carriers at low frequency (Sorenson, 1991). Although this model has encouraged the appearance of a second wave of start-up carriers during the 1990s, none has yet managed to replicate Southwest's success, partly because the strategy can work only in high-volume markets with a sufficiency of airport capacity. A highly efficient, profitable charter sector catering for leisure travellers constitutes a final factor mitigating against a low-cost entry strategy in many markets, particularly in Europe.

Thus, the segmented nature of the airline product, combined with the need for actual entry, suggests that an entrant, wishing to access profitable high-yield traffic, must compete directly with incumbents. Passenger demand appears to be inelastic with respect to flight frequency and aircraft size; conversely, demand for a given airline in a market appears to be elastic. This means that an increase in an incumbent's frequency of flights in a given market will lead to an even greater incremental share of passengers in that market, even if yield figures do not follow. Passengers are more sensitive to frequency than to aircraft size although turbo-props are not directly competitive with jets (Ghobrial, 1993). Consequently, an entrant has to match or exceed existing provision on frequency, service quality, aircraft type, airport and other marketing benefits including FFPs, all perhaps at lower fares in order to get established in the market. British Midland, one of the few recent successful European market entrants, initially began service on contested routes at the frequencies offered by incumbents and offering an industry-standard cabin service that treated every passenger as business class. Subsequently, the carrier has been forced to amend this policy, introducing separate cabins and retaining lower business fares in order to uphold its market share. Even so, on London Heathrow—Paris CDG, for example, this remains at less than its frequency share, meaning simply that the airline attracts fewer passengers per flight than its Heathrow rivals, BA and Air France. It does operate smaller aircraft, but then these tend to have higher unit costs.

THE STRATEGIC ADVANTAGES OF INCUMBENCY

Thus, airline markets have proved to be much less contestable than was once thought. Furthermore, given that actual market entry is necessary to modify their behaviour, large incumbents can mobilise an array of discriminatory strategies to impede putative competitors, particularly smaller companies (Levine, 1987; Pryke, 1991; G. Williams, 1993). The advantages of incumbency derive from:

(i)   the relationship between network economies, the benefits of size, and the development of hub-and-spoke networks;
(ii)   access to market intelligence and the deployment of marketing devices that enhance brand loyalty;
(iii) vertical linkages with related activities in which competition is highly imperfect, including international markets that remain controlled by bilaterals, and the provision of gates and slots at capacity-restricted airports.

NETWORK ECONOMIES, SIZE AND HUB-AND-SPOKE NETWORKS

The application of contestability theory to airline operations generally assumed an industry of independent city-pair markets, thereby failing to take account of the importance for larger incumbents of networking strategies, which can create extensive impediments to entry (Borenstein, 1992a). Significant advantages derive from economies of size in the industry. An 'airline is a complete system and not just a collection of planes. In the airline world, sheer size confers enormous advantages' (Ruppenthal, 1987, p.71). The identification of related economies has produced an extensive if conflicting literature. Many studies have concluded that returns to scale do not exist for airlines, one reason why supporters of deregulation have argued that large carriers are potentially vulnerable to competition from smaller competitors. However, evidence of economies associated with size should not be disregarded simply because researchers have failed statistically to link aggregate size proxy and unit operating costs (Antoniou, 1991). Leaving aside the issue of returns to scale—which must be significant in the context of contracts covering aircraft purchasing, leasing and fuel supply—advantages of size relate to economies of density and, particularly, of scope.

Economies of density are achieved by replacing one unit of production by another: for example, using a larger capacity aircraft rather than a smaller one. If the load factor is maintained, costs per passenger will decline. They can also be achieved through very high utilisation of aircraft in short-haul markets. These economies are open to all carriers and even small airlines may have the necessary fleet mix to achieve them. However, a large fuel-efficient fleet aids realisation of density economies. Furthermore, an airline network is a strategy aimed at maximising such advantages of vehicle size, particularly in combination with the realisation of economies of scope. In airline terms, the latter refer to advantages accruing from the number of cities, or product sub-markets, served. Thus, they forcefully encourage firms to produce over a network which, economically, is more efficient than point-to-point operations.

There are several reasons for this. First, a carrier must base itself at a particular airport, not only for marketing but also because it requires ground support facilities for its aircraft. Secondly, the basic business demand will be concentrated on the morning and evening peaks and, consequently, the carrier has to find other off-peak services. These improve aircraft and personnel utilisation and, unless marginal costs are not recovered, contribute to fixed costs. As complex cross-subsidisation occurs within networks, a seemingly unprofitable route may be considerably more efficient when seen as part of the integrated system (Reynolds-Feighan, 1992). Finally, networks are crucial because the critical mass for airlines is composed of routes as well as passengers. One of the most significant changes in the post-deregulation US airline industry has been the emergence of complex hub-and-spoke systems, which maximise the number of potential on-line connections (same carrier) available to travellers. An airline organises these connections in co-ordinated schedules across a central hub airport that serves as a switching or interchange point for passengers from spoke cities. Because passengers from many connecting destinations can be combined on one flight, these systems allow the airlines to realise economies of density. The network itself is the major economy of scope. Theoretically, on-lining is much more convenient and possibly cheaper than inter-lining (transferring to another carrier for onward travel).

Too many discussions of entry costs in the airline industry have focused on city-pair operations rather than networks. While entry barriers may be low, thereby ensuring few risks for existing firms setting up new routes between cities which they already serve, the quest for economies of density and scope creates an imperative towards network expansion that substantially increases the financial costs of market entry for smaller carriers. An entrant offering only point-to-point service is likely to suffer lower load factors than a competing airline operating the same route from a hub (G. Williams, 1993). Arguably, airlines are seeking monopolies on networks rather than routes, and are prepared to accept some competition so long as their overall network synergies remain relatively unimpaired. It is inescapable that advantages accure to size in these processes.

For example, following US deregulation, some local-service airlines, such as Frontier Airlines at Denver, already organised on hub-and-spoke principles, were able to exploit their lower operating costs to enjoy three or four years of profitable operation. Eventually, however, the largest carriers before deregulation were able to capitalise upon size and protect their markets by re-organising networks around hubs, a process accompanied by merger with and acquisition of local-service carriers. Between 1979–88, the number of hubs in the United States increased from five to around 30. Once a carrier is established at an airport with a hub-and-spoke network—the 'fortress hub'—it becomes very difficult for another carrier, even a major airline, to challenge it there (Hanlon, 1989) (see Chapter 6).

MARKET INTELLIGENCE AND BRAND LOYALTY

Access to market intelligence constitutes a further singular advantage accruing to incumbents, particularly large ones, in turn offering a further strategy that can be mobilised against entrants. This issue has already been discussed in Chapter 2, in particular the influential roles played in consumer behaviour by FFPs and TACOs. Their significance lies in the evidence that the airline which carries the largest share of traffic originating at an airport will be able to attract a disproportionate share of traffic on any particular route emanating from that airport (Borenstein, 1991). This characteristic appears to be attributable to marketing strength and to the development of marketing strategies which encourage brand loyalty. Consequently, an entrant has only two options in the business market. Either it matches or exceeds everything offered by the incumbent or it attempts to target the price-sensitive business market (Grimm and Milloy, 1993).

Clearly, FFPs and TACOs are potentially anti-competitive, part of a battery of devices to increase brand loyalty and limit the effects of competition. As Levine (1987, p.414) argues, 'for a new entrant operating on a scale smaller than the incumbent, the frequent flyer program is a major obstacle rather than a mere marketing detail'. Not only does it encourage brand loyalty, but bonus points can also be offered on any route operated by a new entrant. Such strategies are combined with extensive advertising campaigns which force rivals to respond, thereby raising their entry costs. Established brands, particularly large ones, are also likely to finance public-relations operations, which function specifically to compromise a rival's ability to compete (Gregory, 1994). Finally, brand loyalty is promoted by what Levine (1987) refers to as the economies of information involved, the consumer—or agent—being able to economise on search costs by using the airline with familiar gates, check-ins and procedures. Thus, a large measure of consumer inertia favours incumbency.

VERTICAL LINKAGES WITH RELATED ACTIVITIES IN WHICH COMPETITION IS HIGHLY IMPERFECT

Incumbents possess several additional and significant advantages over entrants. Firstly, even if functioning in privatised and deregulated domestic environments, they can derive financial strength from simultaneously operating in international markets, such as the North Atlantic, which remain controlled by government-negotiated bilaterals (Kay and Thompson, 1991). Long-haul international services are much more profitable than short-haul. Therefore, a short-haul entrant, such as British Midland on its point-to-point

European routes from London Heathrow, has to have significantly lower costs, just to compete on even terms with the global networks of competitors like BA, which has substantially more potential for cross-subsidisation within its network.

Secondly, incumbents benefit from pre-existing access to scarce infrastructure, particularly airport slots, terminal facilities and ground-handling services. Competition is going to be imperfect at many of the world's major airports because these are capacity-restricted, most commonly by runway and terminal availability. A landing or take-off slot can best be thought of as 'a moment in time' and is not normally route-specific. Essentially a slot confers a monopoly rent upon its owner. In Europe, slots cannot strictly be sold (although in practice they are). According to IATA and EC regulations, slot allocation should be non-discriminatory, but precedence is given to the carrier which operated the slot in the corresponding previous season. Thus, it is not unknown for an incumbent to continue operating an unprofitable flight, simply to deny slot access to a competitor. In other transport sectors, entrants can overcome this factor if they are prepared to incur the sunk costs required to establish competing terminals. However, unless a city possesses an underused airport, this tactic is not available to an airline entrant (B. Graham, 1990). Even if alternative facilities are available, they are likely to be inferior to those controlled by the incumbents and, further, may be constrained by air traffic control restrictions.

Indeed, these constraints may prevent an incumbent from entering a market at all. At some European airports, slot shortages mean that entry by new carriers is effectively impossible, particularly for higher-frequency short-haul services. While accepting the principle that precedence be given to historic, or grandfather, rights, the EC has decided that 50 per cent of those slots remaining, once such rights have been satisfied at capacity-restricted airports, should be allocated to new entrants. In actuality, however, very few such slots are likely to be available, particularly during morning and evening peaks. Consequently, it is easier for a long-haul carrier (at low frequency), or a charter airline, to obtain slots than is the case for short-haul scheduled airlines requiring peak-period frequency. For example, British Midland, which has adopted an incremental approach to establishing itself as the second-largest operator at Heathrow (15 per cent of slots), has been able to achieve adequate frequencies on several European routes, only by abandoning admittedly loss-making UK domestic services.

Even if an entrant airline succeeds in getting its aircraft on to the ground, there may be insufficient gate and terminal capacity. This constraint to market entry will be exacerbated if—as is often the case in the United States—airlines own the terminals and gates. In 1989, for example, 68 per cent of US airports had no gates at all to lease to new entrants (Dempsey, 1989b). The failure of the Australian carrier, Compass Airlines (I) in 1991, was partially attributable to the refusal of the incumbents, Ansett and Australian, to provide (despite government pressure) gates at their terminals, including the most important at Sydney and Melbourne. Compass claimed that this tactic forced it to use aircraft which were too large for the market. This constraint is less important when—as is normally the case in Europe—terminals are owned by the airport operators. However, their income derives primarily from aircraft movements, the charges for which may weigh more heavily upon the smaller aircraft that entrants might use.

Assuming that the entrant does gain access to airports and their terminals, a further barrier may arise from ground-handling arrangements. At many airports, there may only be two or three approved ground service agencies, often other airlines, which are in a position to obtain privileged access to commercial information on their rivals' load factors and even yields. New market entrants may be forced to employ a rival to handle baggage and passengers (Barrett, 1992). In some instances, as at Frankfurt, Hamburg and Spanish airports, ground handling monopolies raise serious questions concerning costs and competition.

ADDITIONAL BARRIERS TO MARKET ENTRY

Given this formidable array of advantage, which in turn provides incumbents with various strategies that impede market entry and competition, the dismal track record of smaller entrants, engaging larger airlines in head-to-head competition, is unsurprising, even though there is considerable evidence to show that competition increases the size of an individual market. The US deregulatory experience has been accompanied by bankruptcy and merger, while, in Europe, only a handful of entrants have survived to compete directly with the flag-carriers. Smaller entrants are more likely to avoid direct competition, seeking instead niche markets that shield them from the worst effects of competition. Although extending the range of consumer choice, such services may be high-cost monopolies, aimed primarily at the business market. Almost inevitably, they centre on airports or routes, either abandoned by the major carriers as unprofitable or served by them on a limited basis, if at all.

Southwest, which, until recently, concentrated on airports ignored by other major operators, has been the most profitable US airline of the 1990s, and other carriers have attempted to emulate its niche market strategy. None have been so successful. While there is no European equivalent to Southwest, a number of small carriers have developed niche markets, serving hub-bypass or hub-feed routes from secondary airports, unlikely to attract a significant presence from the large carriers. Inevitably, some of these services are provided in conjunction with the major airlines, several independent European regionals operating services under both their own flight codes and those of flag-carriers. But even given the availability of suitable niche markets, which at least avoid the anti-competitive strategies of incumbents, extensive barriers to market entry remain. These will weigh most heavily upon the smaller entrant, attempting to enter a market in competition with other carriers, and least upon the airline that is simply expanding an existing large network. They include: government policy, aircraft costs, product quality, personnel costs, advertising and promotion of services, route development costs and the airport that an entrant might be forced to use.

GOVERNMENT POLICY

Despite the extensive application of pro-competition policies throughout the aviation world, all governments continue to seek the most advantageous terms for their own carriers. Furthermore, although many bilaterals now permit open entry, some international routes remain closed to effective competition because of the conditions included in ASAs. For example, in the long-haul market between Europe and the rest of the world, the bilateral system remains the most serious obstacle to competition (CAA, 1994b). Even if bilaterals do permit multiple designation, entrants may be unable to overcome airport capacity restrictions (see Chapter 10). Furthermore, while legislative conditions may allow competition, its effectiveness is often undermined by price collusion between airlines.

In the past, agencies such as the CAA regulated market entry through route licensing, a process designed to provide a measure of protection to smaller airlines with limited market opportunities. However, on occasions, and irrespective of the reasons for such regulation, this policy constituted an absolute barrier to entry in that airlines were denied route authorities. Furthermore, the actual mechanisms of obtaining a licence imposed an additional burden upon a successful applicant. First, it incurred the actual costs of applying for the licence, assembling its case and attending hearings. Secondly, an airline seeking to enter a route had to release confidential information if the application was contested by the incumbent or another interested party; the incumbent did not necessarily have to reveal similar data. This process could weaken the main weapon of the new entrant, the monopoly of knowledge of its own intentions, and provide an incumbent with further opportunities to raise a potential rival's entry costs (Beesley, 1986). UK airlines also had to satisfy the CAA as to their financial viability, a regulatory barrier that is now the responsibility of the EC. Such assessments are highly confidential and involve no disclosure of figures, but their satisfactory completion remains an unavoidable condition of entry. However, if an airline succeeds, the capital resources to pay creditors are not required and therefore the biggest element in capital risk is not really a sunk cost. In reality, 'it is a hedge against a defect in the knowledge of the market' (Beesley, 1986, p.183).

AIRCRAFT COSTS

The argument that aircraft represent 'capital on wings', capable of being transferred at will from market to market, was fundamental to the theory that the airline industry is characterised by low sunk costs. Aircraft can be obtained relatively easily without substantial capital outlay. Many airlines, both domestic and international, acquire all or most of their fleets from the specialist leasing companies, other airlines and manufacturers. Leasing costs vary substantially, reflecting the negotiating strength of the airline and aircraft availability. Rates will be higher for modern fuel-efficient aircraft, which have lower unit costs.

Although leasing offers real potential savings in entry costs, because it reduces the cost of borrowing capital, it does not remove the need to finance aircraft. Lease payments remain a substantial outlay and, moreover, the airline lacks substantial tangible assets. Again, a carrier seeking to enter a market incurs substantial aircraft-related costs, over and above the amount paid in leasing or purchasing the basic equipment. Nor is the capital on wings' as flexible as ostensibly it might appear. A competitive business market requires a differentiated cabin product in a dedicated scheduled fleet, all presented in a suitable interior and exterior decor, conveying a particular brand image. The aircraft must be comparable with those flown by other airlines, meaning, for example, that a charter carrier cannot simply switch aircraft from leisure to business markets because of different seat configurations, galley arrangements and cabin layouts. Other aircraft-related costs include maintenance although an entrant could contract this out. However, it may be that the only suitable supplier at an airport is a rival carrier.

PRODUCT QUALITY

As observed above, with one or two notable exceptions, cost-leadership strategies of market entry have generally been unsuccessful. Therefore, building and maintaining a reputation for good quality may be a vital part of successful competitive tactics in many markets (Kay and Vickers, 1990). Such a strategy is critical in scheduled air transport because of the segmentation of the market, the dependence of carriers on high-yield customers and the premium placed by the latter upon frequency, incentives and status of the product being offered. Levine (1987) believes that the costs incurred in meeting consumer demands constitute a real barrier to contestability, particularly given market preferences for practices such as FFPs that inhibit competition. Therefore, airlines must invest large amounts of capital into product.

Any airline entering a market in competition with an incumbent is forced to compete on similar terms. The entrant might have lower fares, but it has to offer comparable quality, a problem which the failed British carrier, Air Europe, saw as a significant barrier to entry in its attempt to set up a pan-European network based on London Gatwick during the late 1980s. In the event, despite having costs significantly lower than its competitors, Air Europe's yield relative to route averages 'was even lower than its costs', requiring break-even load factors in excess of 90 per cent, compared to an achieved seat factor of only 60 per cent (quite a good performance for European scheduled flights) (CAA, 1993c, p.133). Questions of product quality apply, even in those instances when an entrant has uncovered a niche market. Business travellers in particular have certain expectations of cabin and ground service, while a hub-feed carrier has to offer a marketing image congruent with that of the onward services to which it is connecting.

Therefore, an airline entering a market in head-to-head competition with an incumbent (or incumbents) cannot simply provide another option on the city-pairing. Nor can it expect to gain a market share by cost-leadership tactics alone. Rather, the entrant must supply a differentiated product, equal or superior to that already provided by incumbents, while achieving a traffic mix commensurate with sustainable load factors. Even if successful entry is achieved, the airline can expect lower market share and poorer yield than its competitors, while it may also have to charge lower prices.

PERSONNEL COSTS

In contrast to the issue of product quality, it might be anticipated that entrant airlines would possess advantages in labour costs, compared to those incurred by incumbents. In the United States, for example, entrants have generally employed non-union labour. However, incumbents soon devised several strategies to deal with this. First, two-tier salary structures, now mostly abandoned, were established at the cost of some strikes. More successfully, services have been transferred to lower-cost regional subsidiaries or sub-contractors. All the major US carriers now control vertically integrated feeder networks of regional airlines, while in response to the competition from Southwest, two airlines have launched low-cost subsidiaries, Continental's ill-fated CALite and Shuttle by United. The major European carriers have adopted similar tactics. For example, BA has set up a lower-cost BA Regional subsidiary, operating services out of Manchester, Birmingham and in Scotland, together with BA (European Operations at Gatwick). It has also concluded franchise agreements with several small carriers which, as BA Express, fly under BA flight codes and offer a BA product but at substantially lower personnel costs. Irrespective of the actual cost of labour, personnel will represent a significant cost (but not a sunk cost) for a small carrier seeking to enter a market. To operate even one small commuter airliner may require four actual crews, who may have to be trained for the particular aircraft type. This last factor may be particularly important if a carrier has to up-grade its aircraft to enter a market, for example from turbo-props to jets.

ADVERTISING AND PROMOTION OF SERVICE

An airline service is a commodity and incumbent carriers derive all the benefits that attach to brand recognition, including economies of information (Levine, 1987). The odds are further stacked against small entrants because size confers marketing strengths. Advertising will have a greater impact per unit of expenditure for an airline that serves many routes from a city than for one that serves few routes (Borenstein, 1991). Further, large carriers simply command greater resources. In 1992, BA spent £123.8m on advertising and promotion, compared to £37.9m spent by all other UK airlines combined (CAA, 1994a).

ROUTE DEVELOPMENT COSTS

Unlike many of the other barriers to entry, the unknown length of time a carrier may have to operate on a route before discovering whether or not it can ever be profitable is a sunk cost—that of uncertainty (McGowan and Seabright, 1989). During this period, an entrant is particularly vulnerable to predatory action by incumbents, including fare cuts and consumer inducements such as increased frequent-flyer points. Further, as effective entry depends on matching frequency, there will be a significant increase in capacity on a route that will further depress its profitability; 'many airlines have pointed to . . . overcapacity as a deterrent to entry' (CAA, 1993c, p.34). It is inevitable that the sunk cost of uncertainty will weigh more heavily upon a smaller carrier lacking a sufficiently developed network to absorb such fixed costs.

AIRPORT THAT A CARRIER MAY BE FORCED TO USE

The theory of the contestable market assumed that entrants would be able to operate on the same airport-pairings. However, this is often not the case, even in the United States, because of the constraints of airport capacity and hub dominance. Although alternative airports constitute the principal niche markets for entrant carriers, the restricted supply of this factor of production constitutes a marked impediment to contestability, forcing carriers to use lesser airports. As a result, they may incur extra costs because those airports may be less attractive to travellers, particularly the high-yield business market. In the United Kingdom, for example, until the Traffic Distribution Rules (TDRs) were changed in 1991, airlines which had not operated from Heathrow before 1977 (in the case of international carriers) and 1986 (for domestic services) were effectively denied access. Thus, they were required to use

Gatwick if they wished to serve London at all. But a London Heathrow service is much more advantageous than one from London Gatwick. In 1990, for example, BA estimated that it obtained 15 per cent more yield per passenger at Heathrow, compared to Gatwick; Virgin claims 20 per cent higher yields at Heathrow. Again, a Gatwick carrier can expect a maximum market share of no more than 25 per cent when operating on a city-pairing against two Heathrow-based carriers. The relaxation of the TDRs has allowed some airlines—mostly long-haul—to transfer services from Gatwick to Heathrow. Virgin has been the principal British beneficiary of this process (B. Graham, 1993a).

CONCLUSIONS

It is clear that entry barriers into airline markets are far more substantial than was originally suggested by the proponents of deregulation and the theory of contestability. Indeed, they are sufficiently prohibitive to deem it unlikely that more than a handful of smaller carriers are ever going successfully to enter specific markets in competition with major incumbents. Start-up carriers may abound, but the rate of failure world-wide is very high. Again, while low-key entry by small regional carriers into under-served niche markets is a valuable extension of air service provision, it does not constitute the dynamic process envisaged by the supporters of deregulation. Generally, therefore, it can be concluded that incumbency defines the balance of power in the airline industry to the extent that even large carriers find it difficult to enter dominated capacity-restricted hub airports. Furthermore, the existence of entry barriers permits those incumbents to operate effective strategies to inhibit or destroy competition.

Dempsey and Goetz (1992, p.216) argue that 'deregulation should not be viewed as an end in itself; it should instead be perceived as a means to [achieving] a more important objective—competition'. Clearly, the logic of the foregoing discussion is that widespread airline competition, defined as several carriers competing head-to-head on fares and service on the same airport-pairings, is not going to emanate from either unfettered deregulation or even controlled liberalisation. Thus, the expectation of what might constitute viable airline competition may require redefinition. Several commentators have suggested that the best hope lies in the removal of the international barriers preventing the mega-carriers from competing with each other. Consequently, the powerful pressures towards oligopolistic concentration in a deregulated airline regime can be translated into a virtue, if the resultant mega-carriers are allowed to compete in all markets at the global scale (Wheatcroft, 1993). This argument is discussed further in Chapter 5.

5 Air Transport, Uneven Development and Globalisation

Transport provision contributes to the differences between places, the economic and social variations and inequality between countries and regions which are part of what is meant by uneven development. This phenomenon exists within a complex matrix of regional and global factors, the relative importance of which are subject to change through time. Different regions and countries possess contrasting relationships with the distribution of money and power that forms the heart of the global economy. Although the relationship between transport infrastructure and uneven development is widely acknowledged, there is less than consensus as to how important the former might be. Generally, it is presented as an enabling or permissive factor, a necessary but not sufficient condition for economic development and social change. In terms of air transport in particular, this relationship is generally presented as little more than an assumption. Very little research has been conducted into the role which the mode plays in explaining the patterns and mitigating the effects of uneven development.

Broadly, the post-war explanation of geographical disparities of wealth and opportunity is contested by four ideologically defined viewpoints (Slater, 1993; 1994). The first, the so-called 'discourse of the West about the rest', is most commonly associated with the work of American economists of modernisation theory, most notably W. W. Rostow. They envisage a dichotomy between traditional and modern societies, a concept that accompanied the Truman Doctrine of a world divided between freedom and liberty on one hand and terror and oppression on the other. In this scenario, development is defined as converting the rest to a Western way of life. Low standards of living persist in the less-developed countries of the Third World because of a development gap that the industrial world can help close with aid and technology.

A second perspective, defined by European social welfare ideas, and most clearly articulated in the Brandt Commission Report (1980), recognises a global power structure in which the world is divided between an industrial 'North' and rural 'South', the poverty of the latter accentuated by its unequal relationships with the North. The development of the South requires a more equitable organisation of international trade and considerable state intervention. However, at much the same time, capitalist institutions, most notably the World Bank, the International Monetary Fund (IMF) and the

Inter-American Development Bank, were reasserting the cardinal importance of economic growth and, particularly, the role of private-sector
investment.

Finally, and in complete contrast, dependency theory is a theoretical product of the South. It contends that underdevelopment is a condition into
which peripheral countries (and regions) have been pushed by more powerful cores. Capital, production and power accumulate in the latter, partly
because they extract surplus from the peripheries. Therefore, Third World
societies cannot emulate international patterns of economic development.
Dependence takes two forms, the first defined by financial subordination
and the imposition of policies of austerity by foreign governments and
institutions. The second concerns dependency within the technological revolution that is the moving force behind new global systems of production.

These conceptualisations help explain the links between air transport and
economic development, although explanatory powers of the models vary
across space. The chapter explores the relationships between the industry
and development against this contested theoretical background, which reflects the mesh of global and regional processes involved. First, the relationship between uneven development and air transport provision is examined
at the global scale. Secondly, it is addressed from the regional perspective,
particularly that of the continuing failure of market economies to reduce
spatial inequalities. Thirdly, the relationships between the provision of air
transport infrastructure and tourism—the economic sector with which it is
most intimately connected—are assessed. Finally, air transport is placed
within the broad context of the globalisation of service industries, one critical manifestation of the new world economic order.

AIR TRANSPORT AND UNEVEN GLOBAL
DEVELOPMENT

In company with other modes, the provision of air transport infrastructure
poses particular problems in development terms. The necessary investment
in underdeveloped areas tends to precede rather than follow development.
Consequently, transport must be an enabling factor, which may produce
real economic and social benefits, although these are likely to be realised
only in the long term. The traditional view of transport investment as a
catalytic agent in introducing industrialisation and modernisation is now
viewed as too simplistic and even misleading (Cervero, 1992). Rather, the
focus should be on the circumstances warranting such investment (Leinbach, 1989). Transport may be 'an essential element of both the theory and
practice of the spatial development' of a state, a major policy instrument in
national and regional development. However, it is only one of the many
services required for economic development (Leinbach and Sien, 1989, p.3).

The particular contribution of air transport is to be found in international travel, where it can offer major time savings, overcome physical obstacles and generally provide guaranteed access to a country because of the international agreements on air traffic rights. Only rarely is use of airspace absolutely denied, one former example being the prohibition on South African Airways overflying other African countries as part of the international sanctions against apartheid.

At the global scale, several essential ideas underpin transport's permissive role in economic development and social change (Hoyle and Smith, 1992). As observed in the Introduction, transport systems are dynamic entities that cannot be understood apart from the socio-economic, political and historical forces that created them. Secondly, gateways, such as sea- or airports, can act either as generative focal points for development or, conversely, as parasitic insertions enabling resource exploitation by, and profit repatriation to, the developed world. Finally, inter-modal choice is—broadly speaking—restricted in developing countries and much wider in advanced economies. High levels of urbanisation and modal shift are both reflections of societal wealth and are thus also characteristic of advanced economies. The demand for mobility is related directly to GDP and personal income (Owen, 1987), a point of particular significance to air transport which is likely to be the highest-cost mode. As shown in Chapter 1, the global distribution of air transport provision is markedly imbalanced, even more so than that of other public transport modes, which require less investment and serve more frequent travelling needs. The First World and Asia-Pacific account for almost 90 per cent of all international scheduled passenger air traffic, while North America, Europe and the CIS, with 20 per cent of the world's population, are responsible for 70 per cent of all domestic air travel.

THE HISTORICAL DIMENSION

Directionally, intercontinental air routes are dominated by either north–south or east–west flows of passengers and cargo. The ostensible simplicity of this statement conceals the role of the dynamic complex of economic, social and political factors that has shaped the evolution of airline networks from the 1920s onwards. The north–south intercontinental routes largely reflect the former colonial linkages between Europe, Africa and Latin America, the major European carriers still retaining very substantial market penetration into the former colonies of their respective states. The dominant east-west flows comprise the transatlantic connections between Europe and North America, together with Europe–Asia-Pacific and transpacific services. The two axes, north–south and east–west, have very different characteristics.

As discussed in Chapter 1, the development of the major north-south routes began during the 1920s and 1930s, as improvements in air transport technology offered the possibility of more effective communications between imperial states and their former or existing colonies. Again, the development of routes between North and South America reflected the continuing desire of the United States to consolidate its commercial and political dominance over the entire continent. The north–south routes remain dominated by European and North American carriers, the pattern of air service provision, particularly in Africa, reflecting both economic poverty and the unequal balance of power that exists between the airlines of the First and Third Worlds (Sochor, 1991). The indigenous airlines of Africa and, to a lesser extent, South America may have small fleets of often elderly aircraft and operate comparatively few routes. Demand is relatively low and therefore aircraft utilisation is poor. Many carriers are heavily indebted. Third World countries are more likely to be destination points than sources of traffic, and passengers from the First World generally prefer to use their own airlines. For all these reasons, Third World states are in a weak bargaining position when negotiating bilateral agreements. Clearly, there are strong intimations of core-periphery dependence relationships in the geography of north–south airline linkages (see Chapter 13).

To some extent, the east–west intercontinental routes also originated from colonial or neo-colonial connections. The pioneering air routes between Europe and Asia, established during the 1930s, were again initially intended to improve communications between the European imperial powers and their respective colonies. The transpacific routes, first developed by Pan American during the 1930s, were intended to complement the airline's politically oriented domination of US–Latin America services. However, the reconstruction of the post-war Japanese economy, the emergence of the NICs around the West Pacific Rim and the growth of China as a major aviation market mean that, in addition to the European and North American carriers, the east–west routes are now served by an array of powerful Asian-Pacific international carriers (see Chapter 11). Unlike many African operators, these airlines possess very modern fleets and serve both origin and destination points for passengers. They are used as instruments of national economic development, particularly for tourism, by resource-rich states with sustainable demographic structures. The Asian-Pacific states are much less disadvantaged in bilateral negotiations than their African or Latin American counterparts, although many airlines still experience difficulties in gaining sufficient access to US gateways. Thus, many of the east–west international routes are much less diagnostic of core-periphery relationships than are those between north and south. The balance of power is markedly less skewed in favour of First World carriers, even in the cases of India and Pakistan which have not fully shared in the economic success of some countries further east.

To a considerable degree, the orientation of this global network of routes is a reflection of the patterning of the hierarchy of world cities that serve as

Table 5.1. A world city hierarchy

Core countries		Semi-periphery countries	
Primary cities	Secondary cities	Primary cities	Secondary cities
London	Brussels		
Paris	Milan		
Rotterdam	Vienna		
Frankfurt	Madrid		
Zurich			
			Johannesburg
New York	Toronto	Sao Paulo	Buenos Aires
Chicago	Miami		Rio de Janeiro
Los Angeles	Houston		Caracas
	San Francisco		Mexico City
Tokyo	Sydney	Singapore	Hong Kong
			Taipei
			Manila
			Bangkok
			Seoul

Source: Friedmann (1986, p.72).

the gatekeepers of the world service economy (Daniels, 1993). These constitute a set of nodes, joined by a series of linkages including transport flows. World cities are identified by a series of measures including trading, banking, international conventions, location of international organisations and population size (Table 5.1). The degree of concentration of service industries in these cities means that, given the occasional exception, they have become the interconnection points for international airline networks world-wide.

THE RELATIONSHIP BETWEEN AIR TRANSPORT AND DEVELOPMENT

The geographical concentration in the distribution of air service provision emphasises the two contrasting spatial patterns of transport that have emerged during the 20th century (Hoyle and Smith, 1992). First, in the world's richer countries, transport modes in general, and air transport in particular, have increasingly been able to overcome physical barriers and reduce the friction of distance. This trend will continue into the 21st century, accentuated by the telecommunications revolution. Conversely, global inequalities in transport development have never been greater. In contrast to the sophisticated transport systems of Europe, North America and parts of Asia-Pacific, the majority of the world's population remains underprovided with even rudimentary forms of transport.

Transport provision by itself will do little to reduce such inequality; rather it must be part of multi-faceted development programmes. Because air transport among all the transport modes is pre-eminent in overcoming geography and distance, it does play a certain role in social and economic development globally, particularly in the promotion of tourism. However, within the Less Developed Countries (LDCs), other transport modes, which can move people and goods more cheaply and in greater bulk, are likely to demand most investment. LDCs cannot afford sizeable capital resources for aircraft and air transport infrastructure, nor is there likely to be substantial local demand. Immobility and poverty go hand-in-hand. Therefore, it can be argued that Third World airports are more likely to function as parasitic insertions than as generative focuses for development. Thus in Africa, Latin America, the Caribbean and parts of Asia, they may encourage resource exploitation by, and profit repatriation to, the developed world (see Chapter 13).

Outside North America and Europe, the relative importance of an airline and the shape of its route network are likely to be determined by a combination of three factors: the extent of tourism in the carrier's host country; the potential role of that state as a source of migrant labour; and the air cargo market. Arguably, certain of these trends can be depicted as essentially parasitic and thereby indicative of core-periphery relationships. Although the connection between air transport and tourism is dealt with below, one significant point can be made here. Increasingly, the tourism industry is subject to horizontal and vertical integration on a global scale, processes that can cause large leakages of the foreign exchange that is one of the primary motivations in tourism promotion. Airlines serve gateway cities in alliance with international tour companies, hotel chains and car-hire firms. A much cited example of the ensuing parasitic relationships concerns Japanese tourists travelling to other Asian countries whose tour is pre-paid in Japan, who travel on a Japanese airline, stay in a Japanese-owned hotel and consume largely imported food (Walton, 1993). At least in Asia, the destination concerned may itself be a significant point of origin for tourists which helps redress such imbalances. In Africa, much of Latin America and the Caribbean, however, tourist flows are likely to be inward only, suggesting that the bulk of profits is likely to accrue to the developed countries from which tourists originate.

Secondly, because the primary function of the international airline system is to move people, it has assisted extensive short-term relocation of many temporary migrants. Thus, the larger Third World airlines can belong to states that are significant sources of migrant labour. These include North African countries like Morocco, Tunisia and Algeria, which are major exporters of labour to parts of Europe, and Egypt, India and Pakistan which supply workers to the Middle East (Owen, 1987). While these states benefit from the remittances of migrant workers, the latter constitute part of a reserve army of labour, which will be discarded during the periodic recessions that constitute an inescapable part of capitalism. Thus, again, the balance of power lies with the core rather than the periphery.

Thirdly, air transport carries goods as well as people. However, the dominance of Europe, North America and Asia-Pacific is even more apparent for freight than passengers, these three regions accounting for virtually 90 per cent of all scheduled cargo traffic. Therefore, air transport is unlikely to have much significance in freight movement in LDCs, although it can be more important in land-locked countries such as Nepal and Chad or those with fragmented geographies. However, the advent of wide-bodied passenger aircraft with their capacious belly-holds has allowed the development of export food crops from Third World countries, particularly high-value-added perishable fruits and vegetables to be sold in Western supermarkets.

Thus, at the global scale, the balance of power in air transport is skewed in favour of the First World and the NICs. Western carriers dominate the north–south routes, the spatial relationship being core-periphery. In this context, air transport may be largely parasitic. The First World carriers remain very important on the east–west routes, but Japan and the NICs of the Asia-Pacific region have proved capable of developing highly competitive airline industries, aided by the evolution of a very substantial intra-Asian market. These carriers are an essential concomitant to the tourist industry which has emerged as a principal economic sector in most Asian-Pacific countries. Before examining this relationship in more detail, some attention must be given to the ramifications for air transport of the continuing failure of market economics to reduce disparities of wealth and social inequalities at a regional scale.

THE REGIONAL PERSPECTIVE

In many countries, particularly those containing difficult terrain and large or awkwardly shaped land areas, air transport provides one crucially important means of communication for isolated settlements. Consequently, such air routes may be operated as subsidised public services, protected from the market forces engendered by deregulatory aviation policies. In Canada, for example, air services to the Northern Territories were excluded from deregulation, while Article Four of the Third Package on airline liberalisation permits EU Member States to protect designated air routes as public-service obligations. Typically, these include services such as those to the Greek Islands, linking minor peripheral French cities to Paris and connecting the many scattered communities in the islands and northern mainland of Scandinavia. This common requirement that state airlines provide domestic services as a national obligation can be a source of conflict between governments and airlines. Larger carriers are likely to derive most of their revenue from foreign routes, whereas fares on some domestic services will be pegged at uneconomic levels for social and political reasons. Such policies conflict with those directed at fostering a more liberalised, competitive and profit-oriented airline industry.

The continuing need to subsidise this form of air transport provision is indicative of the striking centre–periphery differences in economic and social well-being, which are characteristic of any individual or group of capitalist states. Arguably, systematic forces are at work, the advantages conferred on central regions of any economic unit encouraging the cumulative concentration there of investment, economic activity and population. In contrast, peripheries are significantly disadvantaged by relative inaccessibility and greater distance costs of all kinds. Evidence from advanced capitalist economies, such as those of the EU, suggests that any more equitable balance between regions will occur only through what Myrdal (1957, p.47), refers to as 'created harmony'. He argues that countries become highly integrated, not by market forces, but through 'complex networks of state interferences' into the mosaic of production, competitiveness and employment. It is important to remember, however, that 'periphery' as a geographical description does not necessarily equate with 'periphery' as a synonym for economic backwardness. The spatial patterning of inequality is increasingly a more complex phenomenon, involving lagging peripheral regions that are geographically distant from cores but also more central regions of industrial decline, as well as rural areas dependent on crops that are in over-supply. Equally, economically advanced regions may be located beyond the traditional cores of advanced capitalist states. However, to recognise that a geographical dichotomy of core and periphery oversimplifies the issue is not to deny the spatial polarisation of economic and social welfare that exists in capitalist countries (Dunford, 1993).

The neo-liberal solution to such inequality is to allow the market to work more freely by motivating people to move to more buoyant regions, while encouraging companies to locate in more backward regions to take advantage of factors such as surplus and lower-cost labour. However, it can be argued that contemporary economies, characterised by declining industrial employment, are less likely to require large numbers of unskilled workers, while secondly, there is no evidence to suggest that transnational companies will locate in peripheries to any greater extent than has occurred already. Therefore, Grahl and Teague (1990, p.234) argue that there is 'little prospect that the regional problem can be solved through the creation of markets'.

This is recognised explicitly in the regional policies formulated by many individual states and supranational organisations such as the EU. States create mechanisms of regional transfer of wealth and opportunity for both economic and political reasons. Poor peripheries depress domestic markets and increase intervention costs in social welfare spending. Further economic inequality can create political tensions. Regional policies therefore seek to induce stability and identity by engendering a sense of belonging to the wider state (MacKay, 1993).

The improvement of transport infrastructure constitutes one of the principal strategies of regional development policies, a reflection of the underlying assumption that relative inaccessibility and greater distance costs act as one determinant of the poor economic performance of peripheries. Additionally, there are clear social and political dimensions to such policies. As at the global scale, transport infrastructure is again best visualised as an enabling factor in regional development, its unequal distribution being one of a whole series of determinants of competitiveness. Thus, peripheries are linked to motorway and HST networks and provided with air transport infrastructure, most notably airports. Nevertheless, there is no axiomatic cause–effect relationship between improvements in transport facilities and economic development of peripheral regions. Despite the critical importance of air transport to islands and other detached peripheral regions, relatively little research has been published concerning the relationship between peripherality (as a synonym for economic backwardness) and the provision of air transport. In the EU, a quarter of the population live in the Objective 1 regions, those in which GDP is less than 75 per cent of the EU average (see Chapter 9, Figure 9.1). Community regional disparities in income are twice as high, and unemployment disparities three times worse, than those found in the United States.

As the demand for air transport correlates closely with GDP and income, these and similar regions will generate significantly less air traffic than more central and wealthier areas. Nevertheless, geographically peripheral regions are precisely those that stand to benefit most from the removal of the friction of distance which air transport can provide. However, in assessing the relative importance of air transport to these regions, it is unfortunate that explanations are often couched in little more than common-sense terms. Again, they tend to relate to the movement of people rather than goods. Factors cited in business surveys, for example, include the importance of access to air transport in business location choice (Tomkins and Twomey, 1992) and the need for face-to-face contact in the dissemination of information and maintenance of good customer relations. Within the EU, for example, this means that business people in peripheral regions desire direct air access to national cores, the headquarters of the EC in Brussels and to major financial and business centres such as London, Frankfurt, Paris and Milan.

It has been argued that the classic core-periphery model unduly emphasises the association of distance with transport and communication costs, which, arguably, are becoming less and less important in real terms. Thus, distance and centrality are important only if infrastructural provision is so poor that costs are high (Peschel, 1992). While the latter problem is characteristic of much of the Third World, it is less applicable to developed Western economies. However, this is to underestimate the negativities of peripherality. Generally, peripheral regions do experience greater costs for air travel than do core regions, if only because tariffs will be pegged to distance. Cost may also reflect the degree of competition. Arguably, however, cost is of comparatively minor importance for business travellers who are more concerned with the poor connectivity patterns that increase travelling times to peripheries. Firstly, air services will commonly be less frequent and, secondly, will serve only a restricted number of markets. Consequently, peripheral business travellers will be forced into on-line (or worse, inter-line) connections across hub airports, markedly increasing travel time to important political and economic centres. In the EU, for example, a peripheral city is arguably disadvantaged if it is not serviced by a direct flight to Brussels (see Chapter 9).

Thus, air transport provision in peripheral regions is likely to be characterised by higher travel costs for both business and leisure passengers, poorer connectivity patterns and significant time penalties. These disadvantages form one element in a suite of features that continue to undermine the potential competitiveness of peripheral regions in capitalist economies. The evidence from the UK domestic market suggests that the consumer gains of improved frequency and enhanced tariff structures which result from airline competition can off-set, but not eradicate, these disadvantages (B. Graham, 1990). Nevertheless, the importance of such costs as a deterrent to inward investment to these regions remains unclear, especially if a regime of financial aid is provided to the private sector through regional policies.

AIR TRANSPORT AND TOURISM

For many countries, tourism is an attractive means of promoting economic development, both at national and sub-national scales. Because the strategy is utterly dependent on widespread personal mobility, air transport is one critical element in its successful promotion. The debate on the relative merits of tourism as a development strategy has generated considerable literature. Governments promote tourism for what can be regarded as a series of positive contributions to development. The sector generates foreign-exchange earnings and, because it is labour-intensive, can be a significant source of employment opportunities. By its nature, tourism tends to distribute development into less-developed regions within a country (Williams and Shaw, 1991). Tourism also has important multiplier linkages with other sectors of the economy, of which transport is one.

However, there will also be significant negative effects (Walton, 1993). Vertical integration within the tourist industry can cause large foreign-exchange leakages, while an influx of wealthy foreigners can increase prices for a poorer local population. Tourism can also consume investment, which could be used for more worthwhile development projects, while there are socio-cultural negativities such as degradation of indigenous cultures for entertainment, the habits of foreign visitors and environmental despoliation. Generally, however, governments regard such externalities as being less important than the positive ramifications of tourism development.

Table 5.2. Tourist arrivals from abroad by regions

Region	Arrivals (000s)		Percentage share of world total arrivals		Percentage international tourist arrivals by air
	1980	1991	1980	1991	(1991)
Africa	7 337	15 845	2.55	3.48	36
North America	47 321	74 272	16.44	16.32	40
Caribbean/ Central America/ South America	14 066	37 297	4.89	5.10	58
East Asia/Pacific	20 945	53 892	7.28	11.84	87
Europe	189 830	277 904	65.97	61.06	27
Middle East	5 992	6 712	2.08	1.47	49
South Asia	2 280	3 244	0.79	0.71	80

Source: World Tourism Organization (WTO) (1993, p.5).

All models of international tourism depend on reductions in the real costs of travel, increasing disposable income, widespread car ownership and easily available air transport. The demand for tourism is income-dependent and thus the market is largely restricted to the countries of the First World and the NICs of Asia-Pacific. International tourist movements are dominated by Europe, not surprisingly given political and economic integration within the EU and the large numbers of relatively prosperous people who live adjacent to other countries (Williams and Shaw, 1991). Europe accounts for around 70 per cent of all international tourist arrivals and almost two-thirds of all international tourists (Goodall, 1988).

Outside Europe, North America and the eastern Asia-Pacific region account for most of the remaining international arrivals. Thus, the Middle East, Africa and South Asia attract only around five per cent of all international tourists (Table 5.2). The pattern of tourist arrivals has been relatively static since 1980, excepting the marked growth in the East Asia/Pacific market and the concomitant relative decline in European arrivals. In 1991 (a depressed year because of the effects of the Gulf War), international air transport services carried 36 per cent of all tourist arrivals, this traffic accounting for 60 per cent of all passengers carried on international flights. Wide variations occur in the dependence of regions upon air transport for tourist arrivals, ranging from a low of 27 per cent in Europe to almost 90 per cent in the Caribbean and East Asia/Pacific. Consequently, the latter is both the fastest growing international tourist region and the one most dependent on air transport, factors critically important to the development of its airline industry (see Chapters 11 and 12).

Two specific variants of tourism development depend upon the availability of relatively cheap air transport. First is the intra-European IT or 'package' model, serving either Mediterranean or Alpine resorts. Of the Mediterranean countries, Spain is the principal recipient of foreign tourist arrivals, the most important flows originating in the United Kingdom and Germany (Williams and Shaw, 1994). Nevertheless, the same model, characterised by the availability of low-cost air fares, is also typical of much of the foreign tourist market in Portugal, Greece, Malta, Turkey and Italy. To a large extent, the Caribbean islands and Mexico fulfil the same role for North American tourists. European winter sports or 'Alpine' tourism is also heavily dependent on low-cost air fares (Williams and Shaw, 1991). Secondly, and increasingly influential, is the medium- or long-haul tourist product, typically consumed by Europeans in North and Central America, the Caribbean or Asia-Pacific. North Americans are also a significant element in this market, as are the wealthier citizens of Asian-Pacific countries.

Whichever model applies, price is generally the most important factor in the marketing strategies adopted by the tour operators. Cost is also critical in consumer choice of destination, particularly as many resorts in different countries provide an almost identical tourist experience. The European IT market is increasingly defined by a horizontal integration of operators, as the largest companies move to maximise economies of scale in an industry characterised by very tight profit margins. Further, there is marked vertical integration between tour operators and airlines, particularly in the United Kingdom and Germany. Either airlines own tour companies or, much more commonly, the largest IT companies own airlines. For example, Britannia, Airtours International and Air 2000 are the wholly owned airline subsidiaries of the three largest UK IT operators, Thomson Holidays, Airtours and First Choice. The substantial German charter airline, LTU International Airways (LTU), together with its associate companies LTU Sud and LTE, is also part of an integrated tour operator and airline company.

The intra-European IT market is dominated by these specialist charter carriers. Although similar airlines do exist outside Europe, they are much less important in tourist markets, which are largely served by the scheduled carriers. The crucial problem for the entire IT industry is seasonality. The key to the operation of a successful charter airline lies, not so much in the profits to be made during the summer season, as in minimising winter losses. Equipment can be leased out and staff employed on a part-time basis. Again, the need to improve winter utilisation of aircraft was one motivation for the development of long-or medium-haul charter flights from Europe to South Asia, the West Pacific Rim and Australia.

The advent of the medium- or long-haul tourist model is almost entirely due to reductions in the real cost of air transport. Its development has been aided by commercially driven changes in the international regulations concerning overwater flights by commercial passenger aircraft. Primarily at the behest of Boeing and *Airbus Industrie*, ETOPS (extended-range twin-engine operations) provisions have been relaxed to the point that in the event of an emergency, most large twin-jets are now certified to fly on one engine up to 180 minutes (three hours) from a usable airport. The twins, flying at maximum capacity and minimum seat-pitch, offer tour operators significant cost savings over larger multi-engined aircraft.

The fastest-growing medium-long-haul tourist destinations during the 1980s and 1990s have been East and Southeast Asia—including China which has emerged as a key destination area—and the Pacific. Within this general region, location in relation to the east–west international airline route network is of 'key importance to the growth of tourist arrivals' (Sinclair and Vokes, 1993, p.207). Essentially these routes link European cities with the Asian gateways—Bangkok, Beijing, Hong Kong, Jakarta, Kuala Lumpur, Seoul, Singapore, Taipei and Tokyo. The introduction into service during the 1990s of very long-range aircraft, notably the B747–400 and A340, means that all these cities can be routinely served non-stop from Europe. Australian and New Zealand routes from Europe require one-stop flights, generally transiting through Singapore, Bangkok or Hong Kong. From west to east, the major routes link North America with the same gateway cities, and also with Australia and New Zealand, via Honolulu, Fiji or Tahiti. Many of these transit points have been developed as important stop-over markets for tourists.

Most governments of countries located on these high-frequency routes are strongly committed to tourism development. National airlines, such as Thai International, Singapore International or Malaysian, are key actors in this strategy, spearheading the overseas promotion of their countries, not just within Europe and North America but also throughout Asia-Pacific itself. They are expanding more rapidly than any other airlines in the world, constantly increasing fleet capacity. Meanwhile, through renegotiated bilaterals, Asian governments attempt to expand the range of overseas destinations served by their carriers (see Chapter 11). Thus, the Asian-Pacific states and cities that straddle the major international air routes demonstrate the importance of adequate air transport provision to the successful exploitation of tourism as a development strategy. Not surprisingly, given the preponderance of leisure passengers on medium- and long-haul flights, a markedly positive correlation exists between the major airlines in each global region and the most important tourist origins and destinations.

However, the converse also applies. It is difficult to develop a tourist market in a location that is served only by high-cost and infrequent air services. Therefore, the adequate provision of air transport is virtually a precondition in the promotion of tourism as a development medium. Governments regard the creation or expansion of an indigenous carrier as a necessary strategy to avoid foreign-exchange leakages or repatriation of profit. Consequently, small countries, remote from the major air routes, have invested heavily in transport infrastructure and airlines in order to promote tourist development. Examples include Indian Ocean, Caribbean and

African carriers, including Air Lanka, Air Mauritius, Air Seychelles, Air Jamaica, BWIA International (Trinidad and Tobago) and Kenya Airways. It is an expensive strategy because distances from the principal tourist origins, combined with competition from developed world carriers, require that these airlines be equipped with the most modern aircraft, often expensive very long-range types.

Because of such difficulties, it has been argued that the development of national airlines in these countries may be at odds with the maximisation of net foreign-exchange earnings, widely regarded as a primary objective of tourism policies. This requires that leakages of earnings be minimised, a goal achieved more easily with tourism receipts themselves than those accruing from airline operations. It is claimed that up to 70 per cent of airline income in small developing countries will be lost in maintenance, fuel and personnel costs. While still substantial at around 40 per cent, leakages from main-stream tourism activities are considerably lower. Consequently, assuming that bilaterals allow foreign carriers to serve these destinations, the capital invested in their airlines could be used more productively, for example in hotel development that employs considerably more labour (WTO, 1994). The converse argument, and one still accepted by the governments of most small long-haul tourist destinations, is that an overreliance on foreign car-riers means that services are tailored to the needs of external agencies and the dictates of their airlines. The determinants of demand are metropolitan, and thus few opportunities may exist for Third World host societies to deal directly with the sources of tourist supply (Lea, 1988).

THE GLOBALISATION OF THE AIR TRANSPORT INDUSTRY

As is increasingly the case with all service industries, the geography of air transport cannot be understood without reference to the globalisation of previously discrete national economies. These processes are blurring tradi-tional ideas of geographical identity and scale; as Ó Tuathail (1994) puts it, global and local are merging as the 'glocal'. Slater (1993), drawing on Held (1991), identifies at least three primary consequences. First, processes of economic, political, legal and military interconnectedness are changing the nature of the sovereign state from above. Secondly, local and regional nationalisms are eroding the nation-state from below. Finally, global inter-connectedness creates chains of interlocking political decisions and out-comes among states that, in turn, impact on national political systems.

These characteristics of globalisation are of particular relevance to an international airline industry that remains controlled by bilateral agree-ments, negotiated between sovereign states. Given the ramifications of globalisation, Debbage (1994) for one argues that this system is increasingly an inappropriate and anachronistic method of accommodating the exchange of aviation rights. An investigation of long-haul services from Europe (CAA, 1994b) concludes that multilateral ASAs, negotiated between the EU and other major states, are the only feasible means of organising international air transport, a view that echoes the US strategy of attempting to conclude 'open-skies' ASAs with blocks of like-minded geographically contiguous countries.

To some extent, it could be argued that this commitment to multilateralism is merely following in the wake of decisions already implemented by most of the world's major airlines. The widespread trends towards alliance, merger and acquisition can be interpreted as part of an inevitable globalisation of the industry. It is clear that the world's largest airlines believe that their markets function at precisely this scale, although no single carrier can sustain a global network in its own right. Irrespective of the question of sufficient financial resources, the existing structure of bilateral agreements precludes such an outcome. Consequently, as we have seen, the airlines are engaged in negotiating an ever more complex array of alliances, covering equity shares, code-sharing and other joint ventures. Most commentators estimate that the ultimate outcome of these processes will be a world airline industry, dominated by no more than 12 or 15 major alliances.

While this scenario may define the future of the world airline industry, it must be recognised that alliances are arranged, not from the perspective of consumer welfare, but to benefit carriers through reductions in costs and competition. An integrated global alliance should be technically more efficient and thus have lower production costs than the sum of its constituent parts. Secondly, alliances are a potent means of limiting competition by increasing market power and concentration. Partners will effectively monopolise non-stop services between their respective hubs; and competition is reduced by code-sharing, also an increasingly effective method of circumventing bilateral restrictions. Finally, networks are reorganised so that they become complementary to each other. Thus market protection through the reduction of competition is the very essence of airline alliances. Symbolically, the failed alliance between KLM, SAS, Swissair and Austrian was to have been called *Alcázar*, the Spanish term for an urban citadel. Suboptimal market performance may be the inevitable concomitant of airline consolidation (Youssef and Hansen, 1994).

Successful global networks require alliances of carriers from different continents. A nation's ability to attract major international gateways is a function not just of the global patternings of economic activity but also of the home carrier's ability to become a senior partner in such a network. Oum *et al.* (1993) identify two models for global airline alliances, both motivated by similar processes. The first involves the expensive strategy of a mega-carrier creating an alliance by taking equity shares in several junior partners operating in other countries and continents. The lead carrier is inevitably exposed

Table 5.3. British Airways global alliance, late 1994

Fully-owned subsidiaries[a]	BA Express carriers (all UK)[b]	Carriers with BA shareholding (percentage)	Subsidiaries and affiliates
BA (European Operations at Gatwick)	City Flyer Express	Air Mauritius (12.8) Deutsche BA (49.0)	
BA Regional	Loganair	GB Airways (49.0)[d]	
British Asia	Maersk UK	Qantas (25.0)	Air New Zealand (19.9)
Brymon	Manx		Air Pacific
Caledonian[c]			(Fiji) (10.0)
		TAT France (49.0)	
		USAir (24.6)	USAir Express

[a] In addition, BA has taken over and absorbed British Caledonian (1988) and Dan-Air Services (1992).
[b] BA Express is a franchise system; flights are operated as BA services with BA codes.
[c] Caledonian was sold at the end of 1994.
[d] GB Airways became a BA Express carrier during 1995.

Source: Airline Business (July 1994).

to financial risks deriving from the market performances of those subordinates. The only real example is the global alliance orchestrated by BA (Table 5.3), although the KLM-Northwest grouping has certain similarities. The second model is defined by an alliance between partners in several continents, each of which is supplemented by regional feeder airlines. This is a much less expensive and risky, and thus more popular, strategy, often involving extensive code-sharing. A recent example is the 1994 global code-share alliance between United and Lufthansa. Potentially, this represents the creation of an effective global alliance between two discrete networks. The two carriers operate a total of 3000 daily flights, doubling up on only two routes. Both carriers have also concluded separate agreements with Thai International, although these have yet to be fully implemented. In 1995, Lufthansa also entered into a comprehensive alliance with SAS and virtually completed its global coverage in a separate deal with South African Airways.

Therefore, the world-wide response to liberalisation and deregulation has been the formation of strategic alliances at regional, national and global scales. Such developments are not peculiar to the air transport industry but are characteristic of many other service industries. The competitive advantages to airlines conferred by hubbing—in particular economies of scope—operate in international as well as domestic markets. These economies are playing a critical role in the globalisation of the industry because they encourage carriers to extend the geographical spread of their networks (Put-say, 1992). The logic of the market may point to global airline competition as the most likely outcome of the world-wide deregulatory impulse. Neverthe-less, powerful forces still combine to inhibit this process. These include infrastructure limitations and continuing government protection of national markets through bilateral agreements and restrictions on foreign ownership of airlines. Even if these obstacles could be circumvented, the problem of the fortress hub remains as the principal mechanism through which mega-carriers seek to establish spatial monopolies. Competition between airlines is always going to be a restricted process, not least because any supplier in a market economy will attempt to make it as non-competitive as possible.

CONCLUSIONS

It is very easy to get carried away with the concept of globalisation (Daniels, 1993). Only the largest service firms are engaged in such a strategy, most companies seeing it as a process that they may benefit from indirectly by tapping into the local and national demand created by the behaviour of the largest players. Even these latter remain anchored in domestic markets and circumstances. This conclusion effectively describes the current state of the airline industry, centred as it is on large nationally based carriers, supple-mented by an extensive array of local, regional and national companies, heavily dependent on feeding the fortress hubs operated by the majors. However, the trends towards globalisation still hold serious repercussions for air transport's role at lesser geographical scales. The provision of trans-port infrastructure is one critical enabling factor in economic development; air transport in particular is vital in mobilising tourism as a development strategy. Nevertheless, in comparison to terrestrial modes, air transport is an élitist form of travel, its rate of usage for both leisure and business purposes determined by income. Even within the wealthier countries, geographical variations in the demand for, and supply of, air transport are related to regional disparities in income and wealth.

Thus, the geography of air transport provision is conditioned by wider economic and social processes. Under market forces, air transport networks appear to reinforce core-periphery relationships at both global and regional scales. However, in terms of the contested perspectives on development outlined in the introduction to the chapter, the spatial patternings of the industry's negative effects upon social equity vary widely. In one sense, the relationship between income and air travel implies that air transport is a privileged means of transport that allows cores an unreciprocated access to peripheries. Therefore, air transport can be envisaged as one element pro-moting uneven development and the continuing divergence between rich and poor at global and regional scales. Nevertheless, although air transport does not promote development *per se*, the experience of the NICs around the West Pacific Rim suggests that it is an inseparable concomitant of any development process, largely because the presence of a substantial indigenous carrier helps minimise the extent of economic exploitation by, and leakage of foreign currency to, the wealthiest countries of the First World. In this region at least, the development of air transport has contributed towards a more equitable organisation of international trade. Conversely, the shapes of African and Latin American networks are best explained by the core–periphery flows of dependency theory, a characteristic that calls into question the efficacy of the neo-liberal ideology being imposed upon these regions by institutions such as the World Bank. Such issues are at the core of the discussion in Part Two which examines air transport throughout the world's regions.

Part II